DEVELOPING CREATIVE
& CRITICAL THINKING

AN INTEGRATED APPROACH

Tanguy, Yves.
Multiplication of the Arcs. 1954.
Oil on canvas, 40 × 60".
Collection, The Museum of Modern Art, New York.
Mrs. Simon Guggenheim Fund.

DEVELOPING CREATIVE
& CRITICAL THINKING

AN INTEGRATED APPROACH

Robert Boostrom

University of Southern Indiana

National Textbook Company
NTC a division of *NTC Publishing Group* • Lincolnwood, Illinois USA

Cover illustrations:
Sequence of torus shapes projected from
four-dimensional space provided by Thomas F.
Banchoff and Nicholas Thompson at the
Mathematics Department of Brown University,
Rhode Island. The images were generated on a
Prime PXCL-5500 computer and appeared
originally in *Beyond the Third Dimension* by
Thomas F. Banchoff, published by the Scientific
American Library and distributed by W. H.
Freeman and Co., New York.

Cover design: Linda Snow Shum
Interior design: Karen Christoffersen

1996 Printing

Published by National Textbook Company, a division of NTC Publishing Group.
© 1992 by NTC Publishing Group, 4255 West Touhy Avenue,
Lincolnwood (Chicago), Illinois 60646-1975 U.S.A.
Library of Congress Catalog Card Number 91-60646
6 7 8 9 ML 9 8 7 6 5 4

CONTENTS

This book is dedicated
to my parents
who have always felt that a head should not be used
as just a place to hang a hat.

Acknowledgments

Adler, Jerry. "The Lessons of Rock and Roll: Billy Joel presents history, the album." From NEWSWEEK, January 29, 1990, © 1990, Newsweek, Inc. All rights reserved. Reprinted by permission.

Aldous, J. Ray. Excerpt from *Home & Away*, "Commentary," March/April 1991 issue, Barc Wade, Publisher. Reprinted by permission.

Bono, Edward de. Excerpt from *NEW THINK: The Use of Lateral Thinking in the Generation of New Ideas*. Copyright © 1967 by Edward de Bono. Reprinted by permission of Basic Books, Inc., a division of HarperCollins Publishers.

Dickinson, Emily. "I Died for Beauty" reprinted by permission of the publisher and Trustees of Amherst College from THE POEMS OF EMILY DICKINSON, Thomas H. Johnson, ed., Cambridge, Mass.: The Belknap Press of Harvard University Press. Copyright 1951, © 1955, 1979, 1983 by the President and Fellows of Harvard University.

Kahney, Hank. Excerpt from *Problem Solving: A Cognitive Approach*, Open University Press, 1986. Reprinted by permission.

Landers, Ann. Excerpt from "A Woman of Letters," *Chicago Tribune Magazine*, Oct. 7, 1990. Reprint permission granted by Ann Landers and Creators Syndicate.

Levin, Mary E. and Joel R. Excerpt from "Scientific Mnemonomies," *American Educational Research Journal*, Volume 27, #2, p. 305. Copyright 1991 by the American Educational Research Association. Adapted by permission of the publisher.

Saint-Exupéry, Antoine de. Excerpts from *The Little Prince*, copyright 1943 and renewed 1971 by Harcourt Brace Jovanovich, Inc., reprinted by permission of the publisher.

TIME Magazine. Excerpt from "Doing the Crime, Not the Time," Sept. 11, 1989, copyright 1989 The Time Inc. Magazine Company. Reprinted by permission.

DEVELOPING CREATIVE & CRITICAL THINKING

AN INTEGRATED APPROACH

PART ONE

de Chirico, Giorgio.
The Anxious Journey, 1913.
Oil on canvas, 29¼ × 42″.
Collection, The Museum of Modern Art, New York.
Acquired through the Lillie P. Bliss Bequest.

THINKING
ABOUT
THINKING

What is thinking? Are there different kinds of thinking? Is there anything special a person has to do to think well? Do people learn how to think? Or does it just come naturally? Why does thinking matter? How is thinking related to seeing, hearing, and remembering?

These are some of the questions that will come up as you work on the activities in Part 1. Along the way, you will probably discover that the subject is much more complicated than you realized. You may even have to change some of your ideas about thinking.

For example, what picture comes to mind when you hear the word *thinking*? Do you imagine a serious-faced person sitting in a chair? Do you imagine someone with a wrinkled brow taking a test? Do you say that nothing comes to mind, because thinking cannot be seen?

These are all sensible answers, because the word *thinking* can be used in many different ways. In its broadest sense, thinking is whatever goes on inside your head. In this sense, you are always thinking about something. Some idea or other is always on your mind, even if you are only daydreaming.

In a narrower sense, *thinking* is a matter of bringing to mind things that you can't see or hear. This sort of thinking is different from daydreaming because it involves some effort and it has a goal. You try to recollect events as they actually happened (or as they might actually happen). You put together ideas into an order or a pattern. Telling a story is an example of this kind of thinking.

In a still narrower sense, *thinking* is an expression of beliefs based on evidence. Someone asks you what you *think* about an issue, and you say what you believe. Using this sense of *thinking*, you might say that you think it will rain today because there are dark clouds in the sky. Or you might say that you think George Washington was a great president because you read that in a history book.

Finally, there is the kind of thinking that you do when you are looking for reasons for believing one thing instead of another. When you do this kind of thinking, you look not for *any* evidence, but for *good* evidence. This kind of thinking is sometimes called *reflection*.

Reflection may sound rather quiet and dull, but really it is the most active sort of thinking. It built pyramids in Egypt and sent rockets into space. Reflective thinking invented the wheel and television; it invented electric guitars and music to play on them; it invented baseball and *Hamlet*, computers and Superman. Reflective thinking wrote the Constitution of the United States and settled the American West. Reflective thinking carved Venus de Milo and Mount Rushmore. Reflective thinking discovered the South Pole and learned how to juggle. It moves mountains and investigates how hummingbirds fly. Reflective thinking is what this book is about.

So, if you're ready to go on a fantastic journey, you're ready to start thinking about thinking.

1

REFLECTING

Reflecting is a special kind of thinking. In the first place, it's both *active* and controlled. When ideas pass aimlessly through your head, that is not reflecting. When someone tells you a story and it suddenly brings to mind something that happened to you, that is not reflecting either. Reflecting means focusing your attention. It means weighing, considering, choosing. Suppose you're going home, and when you get there, you turn the knob, the door opens, and you step in. Getting into your home does not require reflection. But now suppose that when you turn the knob, the door does not open. To get into the house, some reflecting is in order. You have to think about what you are going to do. You have to imagine possibilities and consider alternatives.

The second way that reflecting is different from some other kinds of thinking is that it's *persistent*. It requires continuous effort. Suppose you're still trying to get through your front door. You check your pocket for the key. You walk around the house looking for an open window. You go to a phone to call a family member who has a key. Such behavior is evidence of persistent reflective thinking. And if someone asked you what you were doing, you might say that you were trying to figure out how to get into your house. But suppose, instead, you went to a nearby record store and thumbed through the new releases. Someone asked you what you were doing and you said that you were trying to figure out how to get into your house. That would not make sense. You are only reflecting as long as you stick to the problem or task.

The third way that reflecting is different from some other kinds of thinking is that it's *careful*. It aims at making sense. This doesn't mean that reflecting cannot be imaginative. A great deal of reflection could go into writing a science-fiction story about people who can move through solid objects. The ability to walk through walls could make sense in a science-fiction story. But it wouldn't make much sense in trying to get through your locked front door. Such imagining would be a kind of thinking, but it would not be reflection.

Reflection is the kind of thinking that this book is about—thinking that is active, persistent, and careful. This is the kind of thinking that looks for the reasons for believing one thing rather than another, the kind of thinking that asks questions. Socrates believed that it is through this kind of thinking that people shape their lives. He felt that people need to think about what they do and why they do it, about what they believe and why they believe it. He said that a day should never pass without such questions and that a life without such questions is not worth living.

becoming aware

Suppose someone were to ask you what *time* is. You would probably find it not only an odd question but also a difficult one to answer. Saint Augustine asked himself this question. He wrote, "What, then, is time? I know well enough what it is, provided that nobody asks me; but if I am asked what it is and try to explain, I am baffled."

Faced with the same question, you might feel like St. Augustine. You know what it means to be late, and you can set your watch, and you probably have experienced the feeling that time was passing quickly or that it was hardly moving at all. But to define *time* is another matter. It is probably something that you have never thought about. It's something that you take for granted.

Reflecting means not taking things for granted. Of course, you can't ponder all the elements of everyday life. And spending a lot of effort trying to think deep thoughts about difficult, abstract concepts like *time* is probably not going to be worthwhile. You can, however, become aware of what you take for granted. You can, now and then, think hard about things that usually just slip by.

Try reflecting on and then describing an episode from a television series that you regularly watch. Below are some questions you might consider to help you think about the program. Jot down your answers to the questions. Then use the answers to write a paragraph or two telling what you have learned about the program. When you reflect on the program, what do you discover that you hadn't seen before?

Activity 1.1

1. For what sort of people is the program produced? (Paying attention to the commercials can help you think about this question. The people who buy advertising time probably have a good idea who is watching the program. They believe their product will be of interest to the audience. For instance, the name *soap operas* was given to some radio dramas because those programs, which were aimed at homemakers, were often sponsored by soap companies. And cartoon programs aimed at children are often sponsored by toy companies.)

2. Are the main characters people like yourself? Are they people you want to be like?

3. Are the main characters unusual in some way? If so, in what way? Are they unusually attractive? Do they have special skills?

4. If the program is a comedy, what are the jokes about? Is there a laugh track? A live audience? Do you laugh as often as you hear people in the audience laughing? If not, why not?

5. What sorts of problems do the characters in the program have? Are they the same sorts of problems you have?

6. Are the characters in the program richer or poorer than you are?

7. Describe the plot. Does it make sense? Do the characters in the program act the way real people act?

8. Does the program use background music? What sort of music? What does the music contribute to the mood of the program?

9. Try looking at the program without listening to the sound. What do you notice? Try listening to the program without watching the picture. What do you notice?

10. Do you know what is going to happen before it happens or are you surprised? How do you feel when the program ends?

asking questions

A good way to stay out of the rut of taking things for granted is to ask questions. Another way of putting it is that reflection demands curiosity. Your thinking won't take you anywhere unless you really want to find out about something. When your curiosity leads you to start asking questions, then your mind has something to work on.

If you have ever watched babies at play, you know what curiosity is. They poke and pull, twist and taste, squeeze and drop everything they can reach. Without any words, they are constantly asking the question, What is this?

The important thing to remember about curiosity is that it is not something that happens to you; it is something that you *do*. Sure, there are times when curiosity comes more easily than at other times. You may find yourself drawn into something without really knowing why. You hear a siren and look out the window. Or you hear the sounds of an argument on television and turn to see what's going on. Or you pass an accident on the highway and find yourself staring.

But the same powers of concentration that you turn on those events, you can turn on other events. One way to stimulate your curiosity is to begin to ask yourself questions. *How, why, when, where, what*—these are the words used by a curious mind at work.

Activity 1.2

Study the following picture. Turn on your curiosity. Write down as many real questions as you can. "Real questions" are those that try to get at things you are genuinely curious about. You might, for instance, ask questions that begin "What if . . ." or "I wonder why . . ." or "How could . . ." or "What does it mean that. . . ." As you write down your questions, see if you find your curiosity growing. You may even want to write about the picture in order to answer the questions you've raised.

Hart Day Leavitt

seeing again

Something that may come to mind when you hear the word *reflection* is a mirror. In a mirror you see an image of yourself. This sense of the word may seem different from the idea of thinking hard or looking for reasons or asking questions, but the two uses of the word are actually not all that different. When, in your mind, you reflect on something, you are going back over it. You are re-seeing, re-examining, re-considering. Reflection is not so much a matter of inventing new ideas as it is of re-working old ones, of looking close to notice what you missed before.

Activity 1.3

Here is a way that you can use your own writing as a kind of mirror. Do five minutes of focused freewriting. This means that you will write steadily for five minutes on a general topic. While you are writing, do not reread what you have written or stop to make corrections or consider whether you have chosen the right words. For the five minutes while you are writing, you will not evaluate what you have written.

Begin the writing with one of these topics in mind. It does not matter which one you choose. You can select your own topic if you like.

cities	travel
sports	wealth
weather	beauty

When you finish the five minutes of freewriting, go over what you have written. Treat it like a mirror that you are looking into. What questions are raised for you by the freewriting? What does the freewriting tell you about you? You might, as you reflect, ask yourself questions like these:

1. Why did I connect these two ideas?

2. Why did I remember those events or places or people?

3. Why did my writing seem to dry up when I came to this point?

4. How did I feel when I wrote about that?

5. In what ways does this freewriting sound like me? In what ways does it *not* sound like me?

If you find any surprising statements in your freewriting, you might ask yourself questions like these:

6. What am I assuming when I say that?

7. Is that what I really meant to say?

8. What was my reason for saying that?

9. What do I mean when I use that word?

10. How do I know that?

Begin reflecting on your five minutes of focused freewriting by making your own list of questions. Think about how you would answer the questions. Then briefly write about what you have seen in this freewriting mirror that you had never noticed about yourself before.

time to reflect

In the spring of 1845, Henry David Thoreau built a house next to Walden Pond near Boston. He describes it as "a tight shingled and plastered house, ten feet wide by fifteen feet long, and eight-feet posts, with a garret and a closet, a large window on each side, two trapdoors, one door at the end, and a brick fireplace opposite." He even tells exactly how much the house cost him to build—twenty-eight dollars, twelve-and-a-half cents.

At the time, Thoreau was twenty-eight years old. He had been a schoolteacher in nearby Concord until his brother died. After his brother's death, he traveled a bit and worked for a while in the family pencil factory. But he needed a change, and on Independence Day in 1845, he moved into the house he had built in the spring. He lived there alone until September 1847. Seven years later he published the book *Walden*, in which he described how he had lived by himself in the woods. In one of the chapters of the book, Thoreau wrote, "I love a broad margin to my life."

One way to think of this line is to recall how readers often scribble thoughts about what they are reading in the margins of a book. The margin is a place to carry on a conversation with the author. In the margin a reader can pause to reflect.

Thoreau is talking, however, not only about the blank space next to a column of print but about his life as well. What he has in mind is the empty place apart from busyness, the time to sit and watch the world go by, the time to reflect. During those days at Walden Pond, Thoreau took the time to sit and look and think. And in the book *Walden*, he turned over those experiences in his mind to see what they meant. It might be said that *Walden* is what Thoreau scribbled in the margin of his life.

You don't have to build a house in the woods in order to have a broad margin to your life. All you have to do is to look, as Thoreau said, "at what is to be seen," to pay attention to the ordinary.

Activity 1.4

Pick out something ordinary, some object or event from your daily life. It might be a house that you pass every day or a chair that you often sit in. It could be children playing in a park or people waiting in line at a checkout counter of a supermarket. Take the time to look at what is before you. Don't rush your looking. Then write down the results of your reflection. You will probably find that as you write, you become aware of still more things that you didn't notice or didn't think about before. Let these thoughts lead you along. Make the margin to your life a broad one.

You might want to use this activity as the beginning of a journal in which you regularly record your reflections. Thoreau was a great keeper of journals. He wrote thirty-nine volumes of journal entries. *Walden* was drawn from some of those entries.

rethinking

A SUMMARY

When you reflect, you are thinking actively, persistently, and carefully. Instead of taking things for granted, you ask questions about them—even if you think you know them well. Rather than accepting someone else's judgment, you make your own. You approach each experience as though it had never happened before.

To practice this reflective approach to life, you will write a how-to essay. What will make this essay special will be the subject. Most how-to writing deals either with step-by-step instructions (such as how to make a kite or how to put together a bicycle) or with processes that are difficult or complicated, processes with which the reader is likely to be unfamiliar (such as how to do cardiopulmonary resuscitation or how to plan a wedding).

The how-to essay *you* write, however, will deal with something ordinary and familiar, something people commonly do without giving it a second thought. Here are some topics you might either choose from or use to prompt an idea of your own:

> how to eat an ice cream cone on a hot day
>
> how to take a nap
>
> how to sharpen a pencil
>
> how to play a record
>
> how to buy a T-shirt
>
> how to walk on an icy street

As you plan your essay, reflect on the topic. Ask yourself questions about the topic until you begin to see it in a fresh light. Whether your essay is humorous or serious, it should surprise readers. It should show them that there is more to think about in your topic than they ever realized.

II

THE RIGHT ATTITUDE

Good thinking is an attitude. It is a way of reacting to what you see and hear. More than one hundred years ago, English philosopher and essayist John Stuart Mill expressed the attitude this way:

> To question all things—never to turn away from any difficulty; to accept no doctrine either from ourselves or from other people without a rigid scrutiny by negative criticism; letting no fallacy or incoherence, or confusion of thought, step by unperceived; above all to insist upon having the meaning of a word clearly understood before using it, and the meaning of a proposition before assenting to it.

This attitude of clear thinking has two important qualities—openness and attentiveness. *Openness* means not jumping to conclusions too quickly. It means being willing to admit that you don't know something. It also means being willing to look for new ways of thinking and acting. People who are open-minded are willing to listen to others as well as to themselves.

The right attitude is more than just being open, however. You also have to pay *attention*. You have to care about what you think in the same way that you care about what you eat or what you wear. It is because they care that good thinkers insist on clearing up what Mill called "confusion of thought." And it is that eagerness to clear things up, to try to understand, that makes people good thinkers in the first place. They have the right attitude.

knowing what you don't know

The ancient Greek philosopher Socrates is remembered as a great teacher and a great thinker. But in his own time, not everyone shared that opinion. He was put to death by his fellow Athenians who felt that he was dangerous, that he asked too many questions.

Socrates never claimed to be a teacher or a thinker. In fact, he often said that he didn't know anything. And in his conversations with others, he asked such provocative, thoughtful questions that often they too began to think that they did not know anything. One person—a man named Meno— said that the questions of Socrates were like the touch of a stingray: Anyone who came into contact with them was numbed. Meno had often given speeches about virtue, but after talking to Socrates, he said that he didn't even know what virtue was anymore.

The purpose of Socrates' questions was not to make people feel stupid. The purpose was to show them the difference between knowing something and only having an opinion about it. Socrates recognized that people cannot learn anything until they are willing to admit that they do not know.

Activity 2.1

Can you tell when you do not know something? Here is a way to find out. Without looking anything up, write down your answers to the following questions. Then, put a check mark next to the answers that you are sure are correct. Compare the checked answers with the answer key on page 253. Score yourself only on the answers you are certain are correct. Is there anything that you thought you knew, but now you have found you did not know after all?

You might try this same quiz with friends or family members. Chances are you will find out that most people are a little more certain than they should be.

1. True or false? The Emancipation Proclamation freed all the slaves in the United States.

2. If three cats can catch three rats in three minutes, how many cats will be needed to catch one hundred rats in one hundred minutes?

3. True or false? Tornadoes in the Southern Hemisphere spin in a different direction than tornadoes in the Northern Hemisphere.

4. Name four people who have served as President of the United States since the beginning of World War II.

5. In the nursery rhyme, where did Little Jack Horner sit?

6. In what year did the first person walk on the moon?

7. Which is larger—a violin or a viola?

8. Who wrote the play *Hamlet*?

9. True or false? A jet engine moves the plane forward by pushing backwards against the air.

10. How many cards are dealt to each hand in a game of bridge?

11. In a checkers game, how many checkers does each player start with?

12. How many days does it take the earth to travel around the sun?

13. With what profession is Florence Nightingale associated?

14. What was the last state to join the United States?

15. If you roll two dice, what number are you most likely to roll?

16. True or false? If you flip an ordinary penny ten times, and it comes up heads each time, it is almost certain to come up tails on the eleventh flip.

17. What is the boiling temperature of water at sea level?

18. Which of these does *not* dissolve in water: salt, sand, sugar?

19. True or false? In autumn, leaves turn brown because the tree or plant stops making chlorophyll.

20. If you wanted to visit the giant stone Sphinx built about 2550 B.C., where would you go?

21. On which of the following sports teams could a person play the position of center: baseball, hockey, football, soccer?

22. True or false? Like modern reptiles, dinosaurs were egg-laying creatures.

23. Which was invented earlier—the bicycle or the gasoline-powered automobile?

24. How many of the five Great Lakes lie entirely in the United States?

25. What did Benjamin Franklin prove with the famous experiment during which he flew a kite in a thunderstorm?

26. Which takes longer—the time it takes the light of the sun to travel to Earth or the time it takes thunder to travel two miles?

27. When Juliet asks, "Wherefore art thou Romeo?" what does she want to know?

28. Who achieved fame first—Elvis Presley or the Beatles?

29. How many amendments to the U.S. Constitution have been repealed?

30. What is the greenhouse effect?

looking for patterns

When German mathematician Carl Gauss was six years old, his teacher asked the class who could be the first to figure the sum of $1 + 2 + 3 + 4 + 5 + 6 + 7 + 8 + 9 + 10$. A short while later, Carl raised his hand and said that he had figured it out. The rest of the class was still working on the problem, and the teacher was surprised. He checked Carl's answer—55. Sure enough, it was correct. "How did you add the numbers so fast?" the teacher wanted to know.

Carl explained that he didn't need to add the numbers. He could see that the first number plus the last number ($1 + 10$) equals 11. And the second number plus the second-to-last number ($2 + 9$) also equals 11. There are five of these pairs in the problem, and 5 times 11 equals 55.

Six-year-old Gauss showed the right attitude in working out this problem. First, he tried to understand what the problem was really about. With that understanding, he could then find an alternative—a better way of doing the problem than adding the numbers, one to the next.

A similar approach to problem solving was used by a math whiz at a Florida high school. The boy was asked the product of 78 times 142. Before another person could punch in the numbers on a calculator, the boy answered correctly, 11,076. When asked how he figured it out so fast, the boy replied that it was easy. "All I did is multiply 142 by 22 and subtract that from 142 times 100."

His answer may sound silly, like the story of the man who figured out how many cattle were on a ranch by counting their legs and dividing by four. But the boy's method really does make some sense. To multiply 142 by 100 is simple. Just add two zeros to 142—14,200. Since the boy had done enough math problems to know that subtracting 78 from 100 leaves 22, he knew that subtracting the product of 142 times 22 from 14,200 (or 142 × 100) would be the same as multiplying 142 by 78. He probably thought that multiplying any number by 22 is easier than multiplying it by 78.

This method of computation may not be one that you would use, but it makes sense of the problem and for some people it works. And that is what matters when you think of an alternative approach: *Does it make sense?* and *Does it work for you?*

Activity 2.2

Here are some situations in which you can look for alternatives. In each situation, try to understand what the problem really is, and then think of ways of solving the problem that would work for you.

1. Here is a problem similar to the one Gauss solved. How can you use his method to solve this problem?

    $$15 + 16 + 17 + 18 + 19 + 20 + 21 + 22 + 23$$

2. Suppose you are camping in the wild. You don't have a watch or a clock, but you want to keep track of the time. What could you do?

3. Here is another problem similar to the one Gauss solved, but this one asks you to divide as well as add. If you count the numbers above the line, you may see the answer without doing any adding or dividing. How can the Gauss method help you see the answer to this problem?

    $$\frac{394 + 395 + 396 + 397 + 398 + 399 + 400}{7}$$

4. Suppose you are in a foreign country. You cannot speak or read the language. You want to order a meal in a restaurant. What do you do?

5. You want to buy 33 pens that cost $.45 each, and you have $20. How can you quickly figure out whether you have enough money—without using a calculator? (Hint: How much would 100 pens cost? What fraction of 100 is 33?)

6. A friend of yours gives you a deck of cards and tells you to pick one out. You pick out the three of clubs and show it to your friend. She then dials a phone number. She says, "Hello, I want to talk to the wizard." After a pause, she says, "Hello, is this the wizard?" She waits again and then says, "Here is someone who wants to talk to you." She hands you the phone and a sepulchral voice whispers, "Your card is the three of clubs." How might your friend have done this trick? (Hint: Why does your friend call the wizard on the phone? When you listen to the phone conversation with the wizard, how much of the conversation can you hear?)

paying attention

In many of Agatha Christie's mystery novels, her famous detective Miss Marple speaks of the importance of paying attention to people. She likes to draw them out in conversation and then listen to what they have to say. Miss Marple is a thinker. She is a successful detective not because she drives fast or shoots straight, but because she can figure things out. And a big part of her skill at figuring things out comes from her willingness to pay attention. Miss Marple believes that she can learn the truth by listening carefully to what people say.

In everyday life, too, paying attention is important. Even though you aren't looking for murderers, paying attention to what people say and write can help you figure things out. And that doesn't mean only listening to people who say things you want to hear. It's just as important—perhaps more important—to listen to people you don't agree with.

Paying attention has at least two parts to it. First, you have to allow other people to express their own opinions. You have to side with French philosopher Voltaire, who said, "I disapprove of what you say, but I will defend to the death your right to say it." This is the idea behind the freedom of speech guaranteed in the First Amendment to the Constitution.

The second part of paying attention is more difficult than the first. You have to seriously consider what other people say. Allowing others to say what they think will improve your thinking only if you have another quality besides tolerance—you must also be open-minded. You must be willing to consider that the ideas of others might be just, fair, and true. This does not mean that you have to accept them. Once you understand them, you might view these ideas as wrong and harmful. Then you will reject them. But first you have to understand.

Activity 2.3

To try your hand at paying attention, look through newspapers and magazines for a column or an editorial that you do not agree with. Choose a topic about which you have strong feelings. Then, in two or three paragraphs, restate the opinion expressed in the column or editorial. That is, put the idea into your own words, and make it as convincing as you can.

Another way to try this sort of activity is to look for an editorial or column that expresses ideas you *do* agree with. Then write a short piece in which you take the other side. Try to write a convincing argument for something you don't believe in.

Whichever way you do this activity, you may find that listening to the other side helps you see an issue in a new way.

being thoughtful

Suppose you are the editor of a Washington, D.C., newspaper in 1861. You have arranged for a reporter to interview the nation's newly inaugurated President—Abraham Lincoln. You ask the reporter what questions he will ask during the interview, and he shows you the following list.

1. How does it feel to be President of the United States?

2. What do you and Mary think of living in the White House?

3. How big an issue do you think slavery will be in the years to come?

4. Were you surprised at the way the voting turned out in your election?

5. Would you have wanted more people to have voted for you?

6. Have you thought at all about running for reelection in 1864?

7. Do you think the talk about secession will make it harder for you as President?

8. What advice do you have for boys growing up who might want to be President some day?

9. Why did you decide to grow a beard?

10. Do you think your being so tall will help or hinder you as President?

After reading these questions, you might fire the reporter on the spot and do the interview yourself, because most of these questions are not worth asking.

Consider the first one. A question about how it feels to be President is too vague to elicit an interesting answer. You might ask instead, "What problems worry you most as you begin your term?"

Or consider the third question, which asks how big an issue slavery will be. It sounds like a good question, but the answer is obvious and doesn't tell very much. Of course, slavery will be a very big issue. What you really want to know is what Lincoln thinks he can do about it. Knowing that he has often spoken against slavery, you might ask, "How do you plan to use the office of President to deal with the issue of slavery?"

The problem with the questions as they are written is that they are not shaped by real interest in and knowledge about the subject. They show *idle* curiosity, not *genuine* curiosity. They are the sort of question someone might ask a stranger while passing time waiting for a bus.

If you are not interested in a subject or if you know nothing about it, it's hard to ask good questions. You can think of questions, but they are questions that have obvious answers or questions about things that don't matter very much. To ask good questions about a subject, you need to reflect on *it*, to think actively, persistently, and carefully about *it*. And to do this kind of thinking, you need to direct your attention outside yourself. You need to care about what you are thinking about. If you are going to interview Abraham Lincoln shortly after his inauguration, you need to put yourself in his shoes and imagine what *he* is thinking and feeling and worrying about. Then the questions that you ask will be good ones.

Activity 2.4

To try this sort of thoughtfulness, think of someone you would like to interview. Before you write your questions, find out about the person. Use the information to help you understand the person so that you can ask questions that are worth answering. Then conduct your interview.

Or, if you prefer, you might simply plan an interview. Choose someone famous, someone from history, even a character from literature. Then do some background research. Use the information to spur your curiosity, and let that curiosity lead you to some questions that are worth answering. If you like, you might try answering the questions the way you think the interviewee might answer them.

using expert opinions

Most of what you believe, you take on faith. You have probably never seen bacteria or studied its effects on the human body. But you believe that germs cause disease. Chances are you have never been to Antarctica, but you believe that it is a land of bitter cold and glacial ice and that penguins live there.

And the things you take on faith are not limited to the microscopic and the exotic. Your everyday life depends on your believing what people tell you.

Of course, you don't believe everything that everyone says. You know that some people are dishonest and others are misinformed. The trick is to know which people to believe and when to believe them.

If you have a strange rash on your arm, you don't ask the bagger at the supermarket about it; you ask a doctor. If you have a leaky pipe, you call a plumber, not the police department. If you aren't sure how to handle a personal problem, you ask a friend, not a stranger.

All of this probably seems obvious when the problem is a rash or a leaky pipe. You go to an expert. But sometimes it is not so clear who an expert is. Suppose the question is whether school should be in session year-round instead of for only nine months. Whose views on the matter should you believe? The superintendent's? The teachers'? The students'? A local politician's? A university professor's? How about the views of your Aunt Matilda? Or those of your best friend?

To such a question there will be many answers from many viewpoints. The ones you listen to should be those from credible sources—answers from people who know what they are talking about. You may still find disagreement and not know whom to believe, but at least you will have ideas worth considering carefully.

Activity 2.5

Consider this question: *Should television stations be prevented from broadcasting children's shows that contain violence?*

Which of the following do you think would be credible sources to consult on this question? Why? Which would not be credible sources? Why not? What other sources might be worth consulting? Compare your answers with those of your classmates.

1. a vice president of an advertising agency that sells toys and electronic games

2. a child psychologist

3. a Nobel Prize winner in physics

4. a clerk in a video store

5. a representative from a parenting group

6. a doctor specializing in cancer research

7. a programmer from a television station

8. friends of yours who have little brothers and sisters

9. a police officer who deals with "juveniles"

10. your congressional representative

checking the experts

Listening to the opinions of experts is part of clear thinking. It makes sense to find out what people who have studied a subject have to say about it. But listening to opinions does not always mean accepting them. Even experts can be wrong.

In 1939, Albert Einstein wrote a letter to President Franklin Roosevelt in which he warned Roosevelt that physicists in Germany were doing experiments that could lead to the invention of an awesome weapon. Because Einstein was the foremost theoretical physicist in the world, Roosevelt had to consider the letter carefully. He decided to set up a top-secret research program in the United States—a program that would get ahead of the Germans.

And in 1945 physicists in the United States successfully developed an atomic bomb.

This work wasn't begun solely because of Einstein's letter, however. Roosevelt knew from other sources that the experiments Einstein described really were going on. And he heard from other physicists that the results might lead to what Einstein feared. In other words, when Roosevelt tested Einstein's expert opinion, it checked out.

When you hear an expert opinion, usually you cannot know whether it is accurate and just. After all, the expert knows more about the subject than you do. You can, however, do what Roosevelt did when he received Einstein's letter. You can look for good reasons to accept or reject the expert opinion. You can think about what information you need to help you decide what to believe.

Activity 2.6

A   Suppose that you hear a physician on television. She says that children should not be vaccinated against measles. Measles, she says, is not an especially dangerous disease, but the vaccine is dangerous, with potentially harmful side effects. Also, she says, the vaccine is not effective. A few years after being given the shot, children can get measles anyway.

What information would help you decide whether this doctor's expert opinion checks out? Compare the questions you think are important with those of your classmates.

B   A professor from the education department of a major university claims that her three-week course in test-taking skills can improve students' scores on the SAT by fifty points. What information would help you decide whether you want to take this professor's course? Compare your questions with those of your classmates.

being open

An open mind is not the same as an empty mind. On the contrary, keeping an open mind helps you admit that you are not sure of things. It helps you find alternatives. It allows you to listen to others and to hear their points of view.

But you should also cultivate an openness toward your own ideas. If you are going to use as much of your mind as possible, you need to be aware of your emotional responses to the world around you.

Novelist and short-story writer Dorothy Canfield describes this sort of openness and what it can uncover:

> Everybody knows such occasional hours or days of freshened emotional responses when events that usually pass almost unnoticed, suddenly move you deeply, when a sunset lifts you to exaltation, when a squeaking door throws you into a fit of exasperation, when a clear look of trust in a child's eyes moves you to tears, or an injustice reported in the newspapers to flaming indignation, a good action to a sunny warm love of human nature, a discovered meanness in yourself or another, to despair.

Canfield goes on to say that the difficulty in listening to yourself lies in finding the words to say what you hear. "The daily routine of ordinary life kills off many a vagrant emotion." Everyone is moved by feelings and recollections that seem important and meaningful. But when one tries to tell someone else about them, words fail.

The best hope of preserving these moods and feelings is to do what Canfield did. Let them come. Then go to work on them. Try to find the words, and try again.

Activity 2.7

A If you are keeping a journal or notebook, record in it the bits and pieces of ideas, feelings, and recollections that come to you during the day. Some of what you record might be reactions. Something you see on television or hear on radio or read in a newspaper might spark a thought or a question. If so, write it down.

Other entries in your journal might come from quiet moments, times when you are by yourself and have the time to think.

The things you write in your journal don't have to be polished or clever or long. A few words. A sentence or two. Perhaps a paragraph. Just try to save those moments when you notice or remember something interesting, something special. Look for those moments when, suddenly, you are moved deeply. Suppose, for instance, that you are reading a newspaper and you see a story of famine with a photograph of undernourished children. On the opposite page is an ad for expensive jewelry featuring a beautiful model. You might cut out the pictures and put them in your journal, along with this comment:

> The children and the model are looking at each other, but she doesn't see them. She's too concerned with looking good and having nice things to notice someone who's hungry and dirty.

B Try doing what Canfield did. Reach out and find something ordinary that is significant. Then ask yourself what it is about this moment or object or place or person that is special for you. Why did it move you? What does it mean to you?

When you think you understand your feeling a little better, ask yourself this question: How can I communicate this specialness to someone else? Dorothy Canfield wrote novels and short stories to share her feelings. You might share yours through photographs or music or something you make or build.

Write a paragraph telling how you might share with others the meaning of your experience. Then, if you like, try out your plan. Suppose, for example, that you are sitting in a park when someone drives by and tosses an empty can out the car window. For some reason, that can suddenly become a symbol of all the trash in the world. Here is how you might plan to communicate that feeling:

> I want to make a poster that will show the outline of a person's head. Inside the head will be lots of photographs cut from newspapers and magazines showing trash heaps, litter, oil slicks—all sorts of garbage. The poster will show that people who don't think about the mess they make of the world are making a mess of themselves, too.

rethinking
A   S U M M A R Y

When it comes to thinking, what is the right attitude? Here are some of the important qualities:

- A willingness to say, "I don't know." Until you say that, you can't think reflectively.

- An openness to alternative ways of seeing and doing—alternatives that are based on understanding how things work.

- An interest in the ideas of others that is shown by paying attention to them—even when they don't agree with yours.

- Thoughtfulness, or caring, that is shown by genuine curiosity, not just idle curiosity.

- A desire to find out what other people have done and thought.

- An insistence on getting the best evidence before you make up your mind.

- An openness to your own intuition about things.

To practice this attitude, you will write a dialogue in which two or more characters will be talking. You will write only what they say—no descriptions of what they are doing or of where they are. The characters in this dialogue will not, however, be different people; they will all be you. In other words, what you write will be an inner dialogue—the way you might think through something in your mind.

The subject of your dialogue should be a problem, a question, a puzzle, or an issue that you have mixed feelings about. One character will express one side of your feelings on the subject. Another character will express another side. For instance, your dialogue could be about trying to decide whether you should try out for a school play. One side of you—a character in the dialogue—could be in favor of the idea, saying that it would give you a chance to show off your talent. Another side could argue against the idea, pointing out how hard it could be to learn lines and how embarrassing if you forgot them. And perhaps, even a third character might be involved, one who might say that trying out would be a good idea—but only for a small part.

Use your dialogue to show that one (or more) of the characters has the *right attitude*. That character should be interested in thinking through the subject, rather than in getting the others to agree. That character should raise good questions and listen to what the others have to say. If you can come to a final decision or agreement at the end of the dialogue, fine; but don't force yourself to a conclusion that you don't believe. It may be that there is no easy answer.

III

HAVING A PURPOSE

What's the difference between walking to a grocery store and simply going for a walk? Or between playing catch and throwing someone out at first? Or between reading a novel and reading a test question?

In each case, the difference has less to do with *what* is done than with *why* it is done. To someone watching, you might look the same walking to the grocery store as you look going for a walk. But the purpose of these two kinds of walking is different. The arm motions of someone playing catch and those of a shortstop throwing to first base might be the same, but the purpose is not. Whether you are reading a novel or reading a test question, you have to turn printed letters into meaningful sentences. But you do one kind of reading for fun and the other to show what you have learned.

As you do the activities in this chapter, you'll discover that achieving the purpose of your thinking often takes time. You don't always know what question you're trying to answer. And sometimes, as you think, the question changes. What remains is the need to satisfy your curiosity, the need to understand.

discovering purpose

Do you always know what you are doing?

If you are like most people, the answer is no. Purposes do not always come all at once. Sometimes, you think you know what you're after, only to find out along the way that you've changed your mind.

In 1928, British bacteriologist Alexander Fleming was studying a kind of bacteria called *Staphylococcus*. Some green mold accidentally grew in one of the culture dishes Fleming was using. Rather than throw out the dish because the sample was "ruined," Fleming recorded what he observed. And what he observed changed medicine, for Fleming discovered that an acid in the green mold killed bacteria. Fleming had discovered penicillin. He had not started out to make such a discovery, but the purpose of his research was changed by events.

This sort of finding out what you're doing as you go along is rather common. Many writers have told how they discovered their purpose only as they worked. Asked about her first novel, Mary McCarthy said,

> Those chapters were originally written as short stories. About halfway through, I began to think of them as a unified story. The same character kept reappearing, and so on. I decided finally to call it a novel, in that it does in a sense tell a story, one story. But the first chapters were written without any idea of their being a novel.

For novelist Elizabeth Hardwick, the discovery of purpose is also a natural part of the writing process. She said,

> Things that are vague in the beginning have to be made concrete. Often, what you thought was the creative idea ahead of you vanishes or becomes something else. . . . I don't know what I'm thinking about a particular thing until I have some kind of draft. It's the actual execution that tells me what I want to say, what I always wanted to say when I started.

Chances are that you, too, often discover your goals, your purposes, as you go along. One idea leads to another. The important thing is to recognize that moment when the purpose becomes clear, that moment when you feel you know what you are trying to do. When he realized the significance of penicillin, Fleming stuck with it. When McCarthy saw that her stories hung together as a novel, she worked on the book to make it a novel. She didn't try to see what else she could make of it. She had found what her writing was aiming toward; she had found her purpose.

Activity 3.1

To experience the feeling of discovering a purpose, try this. Leaf through some old newspapers or magazines and cut out whatever strikes you—pictures, words, letters, even shapes.

With the things you cut out—make something. The thing you make should have a message. It should say something. It might be a collage. It could be a card for a friend or relative. It could be a poem. Decide for yourself what you are going to make and what you will use to make it.

As you work, notice how your purpose gradually takes shape. In the beginning, when your purpose is vague, you probably won't have a very good idea about what you are looking for. But if you keep at it, a moment will come when you know what you want to say. When it does, you'll discover that you know what materials you need to make your plan work. Find them, and carry out the plan.

the right tools

If you want to play softball, you seek out certain tools and a certain setting. You get a ball and some bats, maybe some mitts, and something to mark bases with. And you go outdoors to an open area that is fairly flat and not too bumpy with rocks or pitted with holes. Your purpose—playing softball—can't be achieved if you get a stack of clay pots instead of a bat and ball. Your purpose can't be achieved if you try to hold your game in the aisle of a supermarket instead of in an open field.

When the subject is softball, it's obvious that the purpose and the means of achieving the purpose have to fit. When the subject is thinking, however, the importance of the fit between the purpose and the means is not so obvious. What sorts of tools do you need to think? Where do you have to go to think?

The answer to these questions is, of course, "It depends." It depends on what you are thinking about. If you are thinking about how to fix a car's transmission, then you will need to have the car, mechanic's tools, and maybe a manual. And you will probably do your best thinking in a garage. For a different purpose—say, thinking about whether you want to see a movie on Friday night—you will do your thinking differently.

What about the sort of thinking that you have to do for school? What tools and setting fit the purpose of writing an essay or solving a set of math problems? You may think you can do these things in any environment, but people who write for a living say that they need things just so in order to do their best work.

Some writers, for instance, say that they have to work in the morning. Some say that they have to work standing up. Some have to write on long, yellow pads. Others scribble notes on wall-sized pieces of paper. When Rebecca West, English novelist and journalist, was asked if she used a pencil, rather than a typewriter, to do her writing, she replied, "When anything important has to be written, yes. I think your hand concentrates for you."

Some writers find that their ways of working change over time. When she was asked if she ever dictated her work, American novelist Joyce Carol Oates said,

> No, oddly enough I've written my last several novels in longhand first. I had an enormous, rather frightening stack of pages and notes for *The Assassins,* probably eight hundred pages—or was it closer to a thousand? It alarms me to remember. *Childwold* needed to be written in longhand, of course. And now everything finds its initial expression in longhand and the typewriter has become a rather alien thing—a thing of impersonality. My first novels were all written on a typewriter: first draft straight through, then revisions, then final draft. But I can't do that any longer.

The environment in which writers work also seems to be important to them. Novelist and short-story writer Katherine Anne Porter said she liked to be alone and uninterrupted to do her work.

> All that time in Connecticut, I kept myself free for work; no telephone, no visitors—oh, I really lived like a hermit, everything but being fed through a grate! . . . I prefer to get up very early in the morning and work, I don't want to speak to anybody or see anybody. Perfect silence.

Activity 3.2

Just as writers develop habits that help them achieve their purposes, so can you arrange your environment to achieve your purposes.

Begin by listing the different kinds of schoolwork that you do. Next to each item on the list, describe the environment. When you do schoolwork, where do you do it? How does the room look? How does it sound? What tools do you use? Do you sit or stand or lie?

Include on the list how easy or difficult it is to do the schoolwork, along with how well you do it.

After you have added to the list for several days, look it over. Using the list, write a paragraph that describes how you do your thinking for school. In the paragraph, answer this question: Do the tools and settings fit my purpose?

When you finish this paragraph, you might consider rearranging your environment so that you can better achieve your purpose.

flexibility

How do you know what the purpose of something is?

This may seem like an easy question. The purpose is what the thing is made for. Right? The purpose of a chair is to sit in, and the purpose of a grocery bag is to carry groceries. All you have to do to recognize these purposes is to look at a chair or a bag.

But the purpose of a thing is not always so clear-cut. A chair can be used as firewood, and a grocery bag can be turned by a child with some crayons and imagination into a monster mask.

Finding an unusual purpose for an ordinary object is one of the basic elements of comedy. It is used, for example, in the movie *One, Two, Three*. This movie, released in 1961, tells the wild story of an American business executive working in the then-divided city of Berlin. One of the targets of the movie is the way the East Germans do things. In one scene, a young man is interrogated by the East Germans, who find an unusual way of breaking down his will. They play over and over again a song that was popular at the time—"Itsy Bitsy Teenie Weenie Yellow Polkadot Bikini." This "torture" is more than the young man can endure.

Another example of an unusual purpose for an ordinary object appears in a cartoon made in the 1940s featuring Porky Pig. In it, Porky becomes a reluctant baby-sitter. Before leaving her child, the mother gives Porky a large book about child care and advises him to use the book if he has any trouble with her boy. Porky, of course, has lots of trouble, but nothing he reads in the book is of any help at all. At the end of the cartoon, the mother returns and asks Porky why he did not use the book. She then shows him what she means by "using the book" when she turns her baby over her knee and spanks him with the book.

Both the East Germans' use of the pop song and the mother's use of the book illustrate the same point. Things—songs, books, chairs, grocery bags, you name it—do not have purposes. Only people have purposes. That is, only people decide how things will be used and what they will be used for. A song can be something to dance to, something to drive someone crazy, something to make people laugh. A book can be a source of information or entertainment, or a weapon.

Unless you are a comedy writer, you will probably not spend much time trying to find unusual purposes for ordinary objects. But being aware of purposes can play a part in your everyday thinking. If you become aware of how you are using things, you may not only learn something about yourself but also learn how to be more flexible in your thinking.

Activity 3.3

Here is a list of ordinary things. Write down some of the purposes that you might have for each item on the list. See how many purposes you can come up with for each item. When you finish, compare the purposes you thought of with those of your classmates.

a record	a television	a newspaper
a book	a pencil	a tree
a grocery bag	a flower	a sock
an oatmeal container	a paper cup	a smile

purpose makes meaning

Compare the following questions.

1. What is the capital of Texas?

2. What has hands but no arms and a face but no mouth, and can run but has no feet?

Whether you know the answer to either question, you certainly recognize that the purpose of each is different. One requests information; the other aims to entertain. Along with these different purposes go different ways of dealing with the questions.

The first question asks you to remember something that you may have learned in the past. If you did not learn this information, then you would have to look it up, because you cannot guess what the answer is.

The second question is a riddle. It is supposed to be tricky, clever, and perhaps humorous. Coming up with the answer does not call for you to remember something that you learned in the past. And you cannot look up the answer. Instead, you need to figure out how the words can be interpreted so that they make more sense.

In some situations—such as taking a test, answering a riddle, solving a murder mystery, or playing a game—the purpose is built into the situation. You know ahead of time how you're supposed to think about a test, a riddle, a murder mystery, or a game. You don't have to think about your purpose or try to figure out what the point is.

In many situations, however, your purpose is not so clear-cut. Often, you have to decide what to make of something you read or hear. Suppose, for instance, a friend shows you this map and says, "Take a look at this."

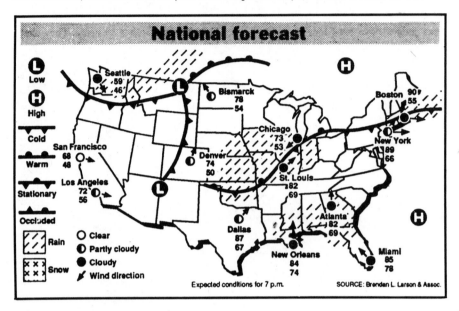

Reprinted by permission of the *Chicago Sun-Times*

You recognize that the map is a weather map, but what would you make of it? Is there something about it your friend expects you to notice? Is it odd or surprising in some way? Does your friend expect you to use the information?

Without having a purpose, you can't think about the map—or even look at it—very effectively. Information, numbers, and data don't make a point by themselves. They have to be interpreted. They have to be used with a purpose in mind. And because information can be used with more than one purpose, it can be interpreted in more than one way. What the information "says" depends on how it is used.

Activity 3.4

Think of a way that you could use the information about auto sales shown in the charts on the next page. Answering the questions that follow will help you to make your plan.

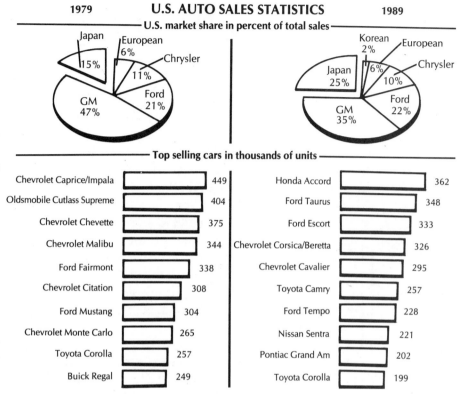

1979   **U.S. AUTO SALES STATISTICS**   **1989**

— U.S. market share in percent of total sales —

1979 pie chart: Japan 15%, European 6%, Chrysler 11%, Ford 21%, GM 47%

1989 pie chart: Korean 2%, European 6%, Japan 25%, Chrysler 10%, Ford 22%, GM 35%

— Top selling cars in thousands of units —

1979	units	1989	units
Chevrolet Caprice/Impala	449	Honda Accord	362
Oldsmobile Cutlass Supreme	404	Ford Taurus	348
Chevrolet Chevette	375	Ford Escort	333
Chevrolet Malibu	344	Chevrolet Corsica/Beretta	326
Ford Fairmont	338	Chevrolet Cavalier	295
Chevrolet Citation	308	Toyota Camry	257
Ford Mustang	304	Ford Tempo	228
Chevrolet Monte Carlo	265	Nissan Sentra	221
Toyota Corolla	257	Pontiac Grand Am	202
Buick Regal	249	Toyota Corolla	199

Source of data: Ford Motor Company and Wards Automotive Reports.

1. Where will you use the information? In an idea for a car advertisement? In a letter to car manufacturers? In a speech about the American economy? In a short story about a car dealer?

2. What point can you make? Do you have something to say about the way cars are made? The way they look? The way they are sold? The way people feel about cars?

3. To whom would you make your point? Do you have something to say to customers? To American car manufacturers? To Japanese car manufacturers? To automotive designers? To advertisers? To car lovers?

4. What additional information (not shown in the chart) would help you better make your point?

   Write your answers to the questions. Compare your ideas for using the information in the chart with those of your classmates. See how many different ways there are of using this information.

rethinking

A   S U M M A R Y

In general terms, the purpose of reflecting is always the same. When you are reflecting, you are trying to understand something, trying to satisfy your curiosity.

Often, however, you may not be entirely clear about how to achieve this purpose. You may not know exactly what you want to find out. Only as you work on a project—as your thinking takes concrete shape—do you really understand what your purpose is.

The purpose of reflecting is more than a target you aim at, more than an answer. Purpose is tied in with the things you think about and with how you think about them. The objects and events in your life get their purpose from the ways you see them and use them. Your purpose for this textbook, for instance, depends on what you think it is good for and how you can use it. But as you use it, you may come to see the book differently, and its purpose will change.

To practice the shaping of a purpose, you will write an autobiographical sketch. This sketch will tell the story of something that you did or something that happened to you. The story does not have to be long or dramatic, but it should have two qualities:

1. What happens in the story should be meaningful to you. It should be something that has affected your life in some way. It might tell, for instance, how someone you did not like at first later became a friend. Or, it could tell how you began and have continued to play lead guitar in a band.

2. The sketch should show how the meaning of the events—their purpose—has become clear to you over time. Perhaps you thought that working with Clarissa on that report for social studies was going to be horrible. But when the report turned out so well, you began to see that working with her had been a good way to learn what sort of person she is.

In short, your sketch should tell how an event or a situation that seemed at the time to have one clear-cut purpose turned out to have a surprisingly different meaning.

IV

SELECTING
STRATEGIES

Imagine yourself performing a science experiment for a group of second graders. They watch as you add one liter of water whose temperature is 10°Centigrade to a second liter of water, also at 10°C. You ask the children, "Now what is the temperature of the water?" Chances are that many of them will say, "20°C."

The reason for this is that seven- and eight-year-olds are working so hard to learn *how* to add numbers together that they don't always recognize *when* they should be using a different strategy. There are times when numbers need to be added and times when adding makes no sense. Composing a song, for example, calls for different thinking strategies than does figuring out what's wrong with a car engine that stalls.

Flexibility in thinking—the ability to use different strategies and to recognize when to use them—is one of the marks of a good thinker. Without this flexibility, you can find yourself using strategies that don't fit the task.

In this chapter you will work with three thinking strategies. The first is one you use when you need to pull together a lot of facts, examples, or ideas. The second strategy is one you use when you need to see things in a new way or from a different point of view. The third strategy is one you use when you need to find a procedure, a way of organizing your approach. Learning to use these strategies and when to use them can keep your thinking flexible.

gathering facts

A common—and often deadly—disease of the nineteenth century was cholera. It was a terrifying disease because the painful symptoms came without warning. A person could be healthy in the morning; stricken with cramps, diarrhea, and vomiting in the afternoon; and dead by night. When cholera appeared in a city, thousands died.

Many people offered theories for how cholera was transmitted. One person was a London doctor named John Snow, and during a cholera epidemic in London in 1854, Snow set about proving his theory. At the time, London was served by two water companies. One, the Lambeth Company, drew its water from the Thames River above London. The other, the Southwark and Vauxhall Company, drew its water from the Thames downstream of London. Snow kept records that showed which water company served each cholera victim. His records showed that customers of the Southwark and Vauxhall Company were far likelier to get cholera than were customers of the Lambeth Company. By collecting this information, Snow was able to convince people that sewage from London was contaminating the water delivered by the Southwark and Vauxhall Company. More important, he showed that clean water was the key to preventing the spread of cholera.

The strategy that Snow used to show how cholera is transmitted was to gather a body of facts. This is one of the basic strategies of reflective thinking—to gather facts, examples, ideas. If, for instance, you want to know what people think about an issue, you need to gather opinions. If you want to know the best place to buy a television set, you need to gather information about prices, features, and service. If you want to write a book about the Aztecs, you need to gather interesting and accurate information. You can't convincingly show the cause of cholera, accurately state public opinion, wisely buy a television set, or informatively write about the Aztecs until you pull together facts, examples, and ideas.

Gathering is a reflective thinking strategy that can be methodical—the way that Dr. Snow gathered his facts—or it can be unplanned—the way that people brainstorm. When a group of people brainstorm, they write down everything anyone in the group says. Then, they begin to sift through the ideas. However you gather your facts, examples, and ideas, the point of gathering is to provide material for reflective thinking.

Activity 4.1

A What facts, examples, and ideas would you need to gather to think reflectively about each of the following?

- The need for new nutritional information on food packaging
- Whether to permit a toxic waste site to be built in your neighborhood
- How students feel about having a dress code at your school
- Where you would like to go on your next vacation

B Suppose that you are working for a small advertising agency and your client is a neighborhood business. (Choose a place you are familiar with, such as your local supermarket, florist, or service station.) Your job is to come up with some slogans or catchy phrases that can be used in radio commercials. Begin by gathering what you know about the business—especially reasons that someone might have for patronizing it. Brainstorm, either on your own or with a small group of classmates, to gather ideas. Then use what you have gathered to help you write at least three slogans.

a new point of view

Figures 1, 2, and 3 on the next page have something in common. What you see in each figure depends on the way you look at it. Take Figure 1. What do you see? A group of irregular black shapes? If so, then focus on the white spaces between the black shapes. If you look at the spaces, you will see a word.

Now look at Figure 2. You may see nothing in it except some black, gray, and white squares. And taking a closer look won't help. But if you catch the picture out of the corner of your eye, or if you look at it from about ten feet away, chances are you will see a familiar face.

Now, what do you see when you look at Figure 3? You may see a beautiful young woman with a plumed hat turned away from you. Or, you may see an older woman with a long nose and pointed chin. The young woman's cheek and chin form the older woman's nose. A necklace on the young woman is the older woman's mouth.

Seeing in different ways is not something that happens only when you use your eyes. You also see things—or understand them—with your mind.

Figure 1

Figure 3

Figure 2

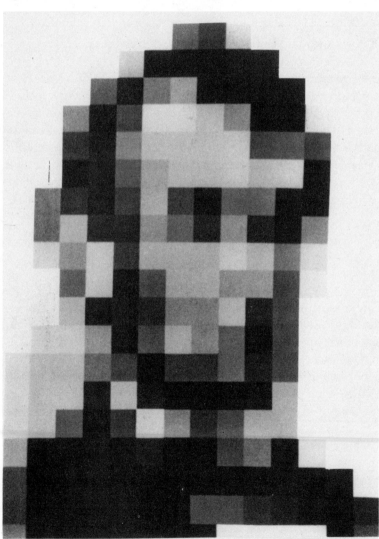

Bell Laboratories/AT&T Archives

And this kind of seeing can change just as the way you saw the figures changed.

Trying to see things differently—or at least being open to seeing them differently—is an important strategy for reflective thinking. When sixteenth-century Polish astronomer Copernicus studied the heavens, he could not make sense of the way the stars and planets moved until he changed his way of seeing. Like everyone else at that time, he believed that the sun and the planets moved around the earth. But what he saw in the sky made more sense if he changed that viewpoint and saw the sun at the center of the system. In time, his way of seeing became the world's way of seeing.

Activity 4.2

A It is possible to draw four straight lines (without lifting your pencil) that will pass through all of the dots in the figure below. How do you do it? (Hint: If you don't see how this is done, you may need to change how you see the figure. Imagine that the space outside the dots is also part of the figure. Your lines do not have to be within the square outlined by the dots.)

B Long Valley High School is financially troubled, and it has been suggested that the school could save money by dropping the football, basketball, and baseball teams. The people in favor of this proposal feel that the teams are too expensive, that not enough students can participate, and that there are more important things for students to learn than how to play these sports.

Suppose you want to convince these people that they should see sports in a different way. How would you do it? Write what you might say to them.

an organizing procedure

Suppose you are given sixteen playing cards—the ace, two, three, and four from each of the four suits. You are challenged to arrange them in a four-by-four arrangement. However, no number or suit can appear more than once in any of the horizontal, vertical, or diagonal rows.

How can you solve this problem?

One approach would be to simply deal the cards out and see what comes up. For instance, your four-by-four arrangement might look like this:

A♠	4◇	A♡	3♣
2♣	3◇	2♡	A◇
3♡	A♣	2◇	4♡
4♠	2♠	4♣	3♠

Looking it over, you see the two aces in the top row and know that one of them must be moved. And there are two diamonds in the diagonal row from top left to bottom right; one of them has to be moved, also. And so on.

The problem with moving individual cards is obvious. There are so many cards in wrong places that you would have to move almost every card. And every time you fixed a problem in one row, you'd create a different problem in another row.

How else can you solve this problem?

You could lay down one card at a time, making sure that it fits with whatever cards have already been put in place. For the first eight or ten cards, this would work. But then you would likely come up with an arrangement something like this one:

A♡	3◇	4♠	
3♣		A◇	4♡
4◇	A♣		
		2♣	A♠

It isn't obvious that any card is in the wrong place, but what would you do with, say, the two of hearts? There is no place you can put it.

About now, you might be ready to agree that trial-and-error is not a good way to deal with this problem. You might even be discouraged and feel that it's not worth the effort. But this problem can be solved. And the way to solve it illustrates an important reflective thinking strategy. There are times when you need to find a *procedure* that organizes and makes sense of what you are thinking about.

You could, for example, begin to solve this card problem by dividing the problem into two parts—first, arranging the numbers and then, arranging the suits. What makes the problem hard is trying to think about both at once.

Suppose you are going to arrange only the numbers in the four-by-four square. You know that the four corners have to each be a different number, so you draw a picture to show this. Then, since the four inside numbers also have to be different, you add them to your picture. And now it looks like this:

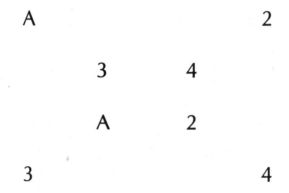

From here, it is easy to fill in the rest of the numbers. Once you finish that, you can use the same procedure to figure out which suits go where.

A problem that seems impossible to solve by trial-and-error turns out to be easy—once you find the right procedure.

Activity 4.3

A If you think you could solve the card problem using trial-and-error, try it. (You can use slips of paper if you don't have playing cards.) When you've had enough, use the procedure described above to complete the solution of the problem.

B The message below is written in a fairly simple code. See if you can crack the code and figure out the message. (Hint: How are the numbers grouped? What do the numbers stand for?)

22–26–24–19 13–6–12–25–22–9 8–7–26–13–23–8 21–12–9
26 15–22–7–7–22–9

rethinking
A SUMMARY

When you face different sorts of reflective thinking tasks, you need to be able to use different strategies.

Sometimes, particularly when you are just starting to think about something, you need a lot of material to work with. At those times, you gather facts, examples, ideas.

In other situations, the problem is not that you don't have material to work with, but that you aren't sure how to put the pieces together. In such a case, it helps to see things in a new way, to change your way of looking at things.

Finally, there are situations or problems that you can handle only by finding a procedure to follow.

To practice these thinking strategies, you will write a letter to your English teacher. In this letter, you will suggest a book that you think should be read as part of the English course. The book should be one that you have read and that you think your classmates should read, too. Your letter should explain why you want the class to read the book as well as how the book will fit with the other things you are doing in English.

Take some time to think before choosing a book to recommend. You might make a list of several possibilities, and then pick one.

As you write this letter, you will be able to use all three thinking strategies discussed in this chapter. First, you will gather ideas about aspects of the book you want to mention. You might make a list of these ideas.

Second, you will try to see the book as your teacher will see it, so that you can make your letter persuasive.

Third, you will follow the procedures used for writing letters.

V

USING YOUR SENSES

Sensing and thinking seem to be two different activities. When you *see* the moon or *hear* a guitar, your senses report what's really there. But when you *think* about the moon or *think* about a guitar, your mind invents something. You can think about a guitar that used to exist or about one that never has existed and never will.

In many ways sensing and thinking are not so different as they seem. Each needs the other. Your senses—seeing, hearing, tasting, smelling, and touching—provide the material with which you think. Without them, there would be nothing for you to think about. Your thinking depends on what your eyes and ears and other senses tell you about the world. However, the ability to recognize how things look, sound, feel, smell, or taste depends on reflective thought. Your ability to hear the difference between a guitar and an automobile engine depends as much on how your mind sorts out sounds as it does on what your ears pick up.

In this chapter, you will look at some of the connections between sensing and thinking. First, you will be reminded that your senses, on their own, are often unreliable. Then you will look at how your point of view shapes what you see and hear. Finally, you will look at how the experience of your senses can be shared with others.

illusions

How good is your eyesight? Check it with the following quiz.

1. How many *f*'s are in the following sentence?

> Frank followed a few of the fellows forward toward the fiery circle at the front of the forum, where Frank fell off the final stair and landed on the flat of his back.

2. Which of the following lines is longer?

A.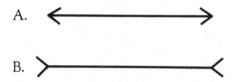

B.

3. Read aloud the message in the triangle.

I

see

the sun's

slowly dying rays

shining the colors of the

the rainbow above the gray horizon.

4. Which of the arrows in the boxes below is the brightest?

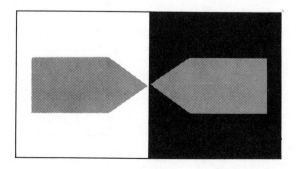

5. Who is the biggest person in the room pictured below?

© 1991, The Exploratorium. Photograph by S. Schwartzenberg.

6. Are the lettered lines parallel to one another?

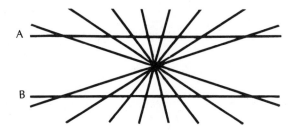

7. If line A was extended, which would be its continuation—B or C?

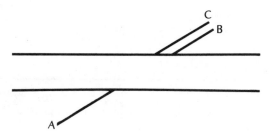

Use the answer key on page 254 to score your performance. If you get them all right, your sense of sight is remarkably keen.

Of course, you realize that this quiz did not test whether you are near-sighted or farsighted or anything of that sort. In fact, if you rely only on your eyes to answer the questions, you will answer all of them wrong. Questions 2, 4, 5, 6, and 7 involve optical illusions. The images trick the eye. Questions 1 and 3 take advantage of the fact that, as a good reader, you don't look at every word, much less every letter, when you read. Your eyes pick up a few clues and your brain fills in the rest.

The point of these tricks is that using your senses effectively requires more than 20/20 vision. Your mind has to evaluate what your senses tell you.

Activity 5.1

A Of all your senses, your sense of taste is probably the least reliable. If you don't believe that, try this taste test. Cut one-half inch cubes of raw onion, carrot, apple, and potato. Put on a blindfold, hold your nose (so you don't get help from your sense of smell), and have someone else mix up the cubes and give them to you one at a time. See if you can tell them apart by taste. (Don't be surprised if you can't.)

B The sense of touch is usually associated with the fingertips, because they are so sensitive. Here is a way you can compare the sensitivity of your fingertips to that of other skin surfaces. Put on a blindfold. Have someone lightly touch one of your fingertips with either the tip of one pencil or the tips of two pencils held about one-half inch apart. Say whether you felt one tip or two. Repeat the test several times to see if your fingertips can tell the difference between one pencil and two pencils. Then try the same test on your forearm, your palm, your chin, your calf, and your back. Where is your sense of touch most sensitive? Where is it least sensitive?

C The information your senses send your brain is always relative. For instance, objects that are close appear larger than objects that are farther away. A whisper sounds louder in a library than on a busy street. Here is a way to show how relative messages can be confusing. You'll need three containers of water—one with cold water, one with hot water, and one with water at room temperature. Simultaneously, put one hand in the cold water and the other in the hot water. Hold them there for about thirty seconds. Then put both hands into the room-temperature water. What messages does your brain get about the temperature of the water?

D Here is another visual illusion. If the spoon were standing straight up in the cup pictured below, which mark on the spoon handle would be even with the rim of the cup? Check your answer with the picture on page 255 of the answer key.

point of view

There's more to using your senses reflectively than just keeping your eyes and ears open. For one thing (as you saw in Activity 5.1), your senses can be fooled. Things aren't always the way they appear.

Also, using your senses means paying attention to some things and ignoring others. You can't pay attention to everything your senses pick up. Think, for example, about how magicians work. They often base illusions on their ability to misdirect people's attention. The *audience* does not choose what it will pay attention to; the *magician* does. Or, consider what happens when witnesses describe an accident. Often, they cannot agree about such basic facts as how tall a person was or what color a car was. The reason for disagreement is usually not faulty vision; the reason is that the witnesses were not paying attention to the person's height or the car's color. Your ability to use your senses is limited to what you notice—what you pay attention to.

What you notice depends, in turn, on your point of view. Both your purposes and your experiences affect how you look at the world and what you see. A hiker who is looking for a place to camp sees the same terrain differently than a landscape painter does. A baker knows more about how bread dough is supposed to feel than does someone who has never kneaded a loaf. A musician is more likely to recognize a wrong note in a band's performance than is someone who is indifferent to music.

Because you can control your purpose and draw on different experiences, you can change your point of view. You can imagine yourself as a hiker or a painter, as a baker or a musician. In one of the great American novels, Mark Twain imagined what it would be like to see the world through the eyes of a young uneducated boy named Huckleberry Finn. In one scene, Huck unexpectedly meets the father he fears and hasn't seen for a year. Here is how Huck describes his father:

> He was most fifty and he looked it. His hair was long and tangled and greasy, and hung down, and you could see his eyes shining through like he was behind vines. It was all black, no gray; so was his long, mixed-up whiskers. There warn't no color in his face, where his face showed; it was white; not like another man's white, but white to make a body sick, a white to make a body's flesh crawl—a tree-toad white, a fish-belly white. As for his clothes—just rags, that was all. He had one ankle resting on 'tother knee; the boot on that foot was busted, and two of his toes stuck through, and he worked them now and then. His hat was laying on the floor; an old black slouch with the top caved in, like a lid.

To observe like this calls for more than looking closely. It calls for imagination. It calls for the ability to fit the information your senses give you to the point of view of someone else.

Activity 5.2

A How unique is your own point of view? Do you notice things that others don't? Here is a way to find out. Along with three or four classmates, pick out a scene to study. It could be something large—an athletic field, an auditorium, a city block. Or it could be something small—a window box, a locker, a shelf of books. Choose something of interest to the members of the group. Then, on your own, study what your group has chosen and list what you observe. Jot down whatever details your senses pick up. When you finish, compare your list to those of your classmates. In what ways is your point of view different from those of your classmates?

B Try taking on a different point of view. First, imagine that you are a three-year-old toddler (a little under three feet tall). Look around the room you are in right now. Make a list of the things you notice. Jot down a note that explains why you noticed each detail on your list. Put your list aside.

Then, imagine that you are an architect who has been hired to remodel the same room. Look around, and make a list of the things you notice. Once again, jot down notes to explain why you notice these things.

Compare your two lists. In what ways are they different? Why?

sense and meaning

Using your senses reflectively involves more than just taking things in. It also involves being able to talk about what you see and hear in a way that makes yours observations meaningful to others.

You do this, of course, with words. Sights and sounds have to be given names. The more precise the words, the more your thinking will benefit from your senses. Calling something a *1962 Pontiac convertible* instead of a *car* not only helps you communicate with others but also helps you be clearer in your own mind.

Another way to help make your observations meaningful is to link them with other experiences. This method is used by Henry David Thoreau in the following passage. Like most of Thoreau's descriptions of what he saw in the woods around Walden Pond, this one is filled with images and ideas.

> One day when I went out to my wood-pile, or rather my pile of stumps, I observed two large ants, the one red, the other much larger, nearly half an inch long, and black, fiercely contending with one another. Having once got hold they they never let go, but struggled and wrestled and rolled on the chips incessantly. Looking farther, I was surprised to find that the chips were covered with such combatants, that it was not a *duellum*, but a *bellum*, war between two races of ants, the red always pitted against the black, and frequently two red ones to one black. The legions of these Myrmidons covered all the hills and vales in my wood-yard, and the ground was already strewn with the dead and dying, both red and black. It was the only battle

which I have ever witnessed, the only battle-field I ever trod while the battle was raging; internecine war; the red republicans on the one hand, and the black imperialists on the other. On every side they were engaged in deadly combat, yet without any noise that I could hear, and human soldiers never fought so resolutely. I watched a couple that were fast locked in each other's embraces, in a little sunny valley amid the chips, now at noonday prepared to fight till the sun went down, or life went out. The smaller red champion had fastened himself like a vise to his adversary's front, and through all the tumblings on that field never for an instant ceased to gnaw at one of his feelers near the root, having already caused the other to go by the board; while the stronger black one dashed him from side to side, and, I saw on looking nearer, had already divested him of several of his members. They fought with more pertinacity than bulldogs. Neither manifested the least disposition to retreat. It was evident that their battle cry was "Conquer or die."

Thoreau used his senses to see what many people would have missed. He was able to share what he saw by using plain, strong words: *red, black, wrestled, rolled, battle, chips, noonday, sun, life, champion, vise, tumblings, gnaw, feelers, root, dashed, fought.* He also made his observations vivid by comparing the battle of the ants to the wars of humans. Through his comparisons and his concrete language, Thoreau is able to communicate both what he saw and, more important, what it meant to him. Instead of seeing some ants in a woodpile, the reader is brought to see suffering and courage.

Activity 5.3

You, too, can find an event like the one Thoreau found—a small event with a large meaning. You need to be alert in using your senses. You need to pay attention. And you probably will have to be patient, giving the event time to unfold. Thoreau watched the ants for an entire afternoon.

Look for such an event. When you find one, turn your senses on it. Study it patiently. Then make a list of words that you would use if you were going to describe the event. Try, in particular, to come up with vigorous, energetic nouns and verbs, as Thoreau did.

When you think you've finished the list, review it. Do the words—even without sentences or explanation—suggest the meaning you saw in the event? If not, perhaps there are other words that need to be on the list. Add them. Then save the list in your notebook.

rethinking

A   S U M M A R Y

You have seen in this chapter some of the connections between sensing and thinking. Each activity depends on the other. Without reflection to guide them, your senses are like a camera with no one to aim and focus it. Reflective thought leads to a point of view that guides your senses. Then, the information provided by your eyes and ears and all your other senses becomes meaningful—something you can share with others.

To practice using your senses reflectively, write a descriptive essay. Imagine that you are an anthropologist, a scientist who studies people in relation to their society. You are studying the way that people in your school, community, or neighborhood live and think.

To prepare for your essay, choose a specific place in which you can observe a specific activity. You might, for instance, watch how people behave in a cafeteria line or in a library.

Once you've chosen your focus, spend some time observing the activity in the place you are studying. Don't assume you already know what you will find. Be open. Look and listen for patterns of behavior. Jot down notes describing what you see and hear. If you are listening to conversations, try to write down the actual words. Make certain, of course, before you eavesdrop, that the people know what you are doing and that you are not intruding on their privacy.

Use your notes to help you recreate the scene in your essay, just as if you were a creature from Mars seeing it all for the first time. Let readers see and hear what you saw and heard. At the same time, show readers the meaning of what you have observed. Draw on the scene to explain how the people you are writing about think and live their lives.

VI

REMEMBERING

What do you think of when you hear the phrase "absentminded professor"? Maybe you imagine someone who is brilliant but forgetful. Someone who can solve the mysteries of the universe but forgets where the car keys are.

The stereotype of the absentminded professor underscores a difference many people believe exists between remembering and thinking. Having a good memory, like being able to carry a tune, seems to have nothing to do with thinking.

Games like Trivial Pursuit and TV shows like "Jeopardy" emphasize the quick recall of a variety of facts. You don't think through a question like "In what country is Transylvania?" Answering such a question isn't like solving a complicated math problem. You either remember the answer or you don't. Right?

Well, yes and no. Sometimes facts and recollections do seem to pop effortlessly into your mind. But remembering is more than recalling where you put things or being able to come up with out-of-the-way facts. Your memory doesn't simply record the world; it classifies, shapes, and structures it. What you remember depends not only on the *what* but also on *you*. Remembering involves imagination and reconstruction. Remembering is part of thinking.

In this chapter, you will look, first, at mnemonic devices—procedures that help people memorize and recall. Then, you will look at the ways in which remembering is like discovery. Finally, you will look at the role of your personal memories in reflective thinking.

mnemonics

Remembering is often like fitting a piece into a jigsaw puzzle. You know the shape of the thing you are looking for; you just have to find it. You search your memory with questions like these:

How do you spell *conceive*?

When did the Civil War begin?

What is Celia's phone number?

What time is the rerun of "Star Trek" on?

What is that tall woman's name?

What ingredients do I need for pancakes?

You may believe that remembering of this sort happens by accident or that some people are just born with a good memory. There is some truth to this. People do recall things they never tried to memorize—just think of all the advertising jingles you have stored in your memory.

It is also true that people's memories work differently. Russian psychologist A. R. Luria wrote a book about a man who couldn't forget. This man, called "S," could memorize long columns of numbers and then recall them years later. S eventually worked as a professional mnemonist—a stage performer who memorizes and recalls things suggested by the audience.

It might sound wonderful to have such a memory, but consider the drawbacks. S remembered all the pains and disappointments of childhood—as freshly as if they had just occurred. Or, suppose that S wanted to remember how an unusual word was spelled. He could do it, of course, if he had ever come across the word in print. But along with the word, he would also see in his mind's eye everything else on the page. In addition, he would remember the color of the book, how heavy it felt in his hand, the room he was sitting in when he held the book, the shape of the chair he was sitting on, the time of day, the weather that day, and on and on. S's problem was not to learn how to remember, but to learn how to forget.

Your problem, however, is probably just the opposite—how to remember. What you need are some mnemonic devices—methods of aiding your memory. There are two basic ways you can make memorizing and recalling easier. One way is to relate what you are memorizing to something you already know. This often involves finding a pattern in what you wish to memorize. For example, which of the following lines could you learn faster and remember longer?

- The dolphin danced on its flippers across the pool.
- its across pool danced flippers the the on dolphin

You'll probably agree that the first is easier to remember. A sentence is easier to memorize than a random list of words because it has a pattern you are familiar with. The other basic way you can aid your memory is to visualize what you're trying to memorize. Here is a picture that shows how you could use visualization to help you remember part of the plant classification system.

To remember that the subdivision <u>gymnosperms</u> includes the class <u>conopsida</u>, which in turn includes the three orders <u>ginkgoales</u>, <u>pinales</u>, and <u>taxales</u>, study the picture of the swinging <u>gymnast</u> with the <u>ice cream cone</u> in his hand. The ice cream is about to splat in the face of the <u>king</u> who is leaping from the bench of his royal <u>piano</u> after sitting on some <u>tacks</u>.

Adapted from an excerpt from "Scientific Mnemonomies" by Mary E. and Joel R. Levin.

Activity 6.1

A   Suppose you are trying to memorize the names of the eight types of bones from the top of the leg to the toes in the foot: femur, patella, tibia, fibula, calcaneus, tarsals, metatarsals, and phalanges. Here is a way you can do it, similar to the way that S remembered things. It uses both a pattern and visualization.

Pick out eight familiar objects that form a path. The objects must be so familiar that you can easily see them in your mind's eye. For instance, you might pick out pieces of furniture in your home, say, a desk, the couch, a television, a lamp, the dining table, a coatrack, a telephone, and the dishwasher. Try to pick objects that are quite different from one another and that follow a path as you move around the room or move from one room to the next. Now, take the first bone, the femur, and imagine it on top of or as part of the first item on your list. You might see the femur as one of the legs of the desk. Then imagine the patella sitting on or as part of the second item on your list. You might imagine it as a couch button. (For help with this imagining, look at the diagrams below to see what these bones look like.) Practice linking the names this way twice today for about fifteen minutes each time. Test yourself tomorrow to see how well you remember the names. Test yourself again in a week to see how well this mnemonic works for you. The same mnemonic device can be used for much longer lists just by adding to your list of objects.

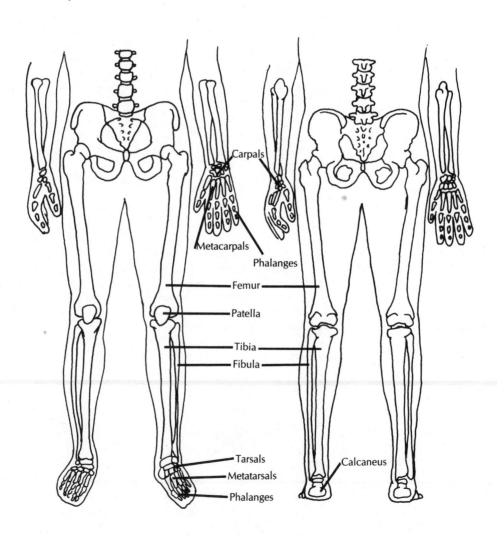

B Questions can help you memorize lists and recall them later. Read the following questions. Then turn to page 63 and study the picture for one minute. Turn back to this page and write your answers to the questions.

1. How many people are in the picture? How many of them are men? How many are standing? How many are sitting? How many are running? How many are lying down?

2. Some of the men are carrying or holding things. What are they carrying or holding?

3. How many of the men are wearing something over their face? What are they wearing? How many of them are wearing hats? How many are wearing leather jackets?

4. What do you think is going on in this picture?

C Memorizing key facts can help you store information. If someone asked you who was President of the United States in 1819, you might have no idea at all, and you might think that being able to hold information like that in your memory would be impossible. However, if you can remember three key facts, you will know who was President every year from 1788 until 1837. Here are the key facts.

1. The first seven presidents were Washington, Adams, Jefferson, Madison, Monroe, Adams, and Jackson.

2. All served two terms as President except the two Adamses.

3. Presidents were elected every four years, beginning in 1788, and began their term of office the year following their election.

Memorize these three key facts. Then have a friend pick any year from 1788 to 1837, and you tell your friend who was President that year.

D A familiar way of storing key facts is to use an easy-to-remember rule. If someone asks, "How do you spell *conceive*?" you might say to yourself, "*i* before *e* except after *c*, or when sounded like *ay*, as in *neighbor* and *weigh*." It is easier to memorize the rule than to memorize all the words with *ie* and *ei* in them. What other rules like this can you think of? (For example, what rule do you use to remember how many days are in a given month?)

E Sometimes, pulling something out of your memory requires a procedure. For instance, many people find it helps, when they are trying to recall someone's name, to think of each letter of the alphabet. The next time you are stumped for someone's name, you might try this mnemonic device and see if it works for you.

discovery

At times, remembering feels like discovering. You know the feeling: You hear a riddle that has you stumped. You give up. Then you are told the answer, and you think, "Of course!" You remember the clues of the riddle; now they make sense.

Finding the solution to a problem often creates this feeling of "Of course!" When the fictional detective Sherlock Holmes is asked by Dr. Watson how he knew that Watson had been in Afghanistan, Holmes replies:

> The train of reasoning ran, "Here is a gentleman of a medical type, but with the air of a military man. Clearly an army doctor then. He has just come from the tropics, for his face is dark, and that is not the natural tint of his skin, for his wrists are fair. He has undergone hardship and sickness, as his haggard face says clearly. His left arm has been injured. He holds it in a stiff and unnatural manner. Where in the tropics could an English army doctor have seen much hardship and got his arm wounded? Clearly in Afghanistan." The whole train of thought did not occupy a second.

Led to the conclusion in this way, Watson is not astonished or surprised. He says, "It is simple enough as you explain it."

The ancient Greek philosopher Socrates said that all learning is actually recollection. People who are puzzled, he said, are really asking themselves questions. As they answer the questions, they begin to solve whatever puzzled them. And the answers are a kind of remembering. This kind of remembering—the discovery kind—is different from, say, remembering someone's address. When you try to remember an address, you know what you are looking for. But with the kind of remembering Socrates talked about, you don't know what you are looking for—not until you discover it, not until you remember.

Suppose, for example, that you want to buy a birthday present for a special friend. You think about it and think about it, and then you remember her telling you how much she's enjoyed painting in her art class. Paints and brushes, you decide, would make a great present. Your problem is solved when you remember your friend's comment, but you didn't know what you were trying to remember until you actually discovered it.

Activity 6.2

A People often know more about a subject than they can easily recall. One way to get at this knowledge is brainstorming. When you brainstorm, you write down whatever ideas come to mind. Often, one idea will lead you unexpectedly to just the idea or fact that you were looking for. Although people usually brainstorm in groups, you can use the same technique to discover ideas in your own memory.

Suppose you have been assigned to write an essay about a scientific invention that has changed people's lives. Chances are good that a topic does not come immediately to mind. But give your memory a chance. Brainstorm for five minutes, jotting down every idea that comes to mind, even those you do not think are very good. Then review your notes. Choose a topic and share it with your classmates. Explain why you think it is a good topic for the assignment.

B If you did Activity 6.1, you can do this remembering exercise. Without looking at the picture at the end of this chapter again, see what you can remember about it. In particular, ask yourself whether the picture portrays an actual robbery or an enactment of a robbery. Use freewriting to help you recall as much as possible. (Don't forget to think about the person who was taking this picture as well as about the people in the shot. Are the people in the picture aware of the photographer?) Mentally focusing on the picture and how you imagine it was taken, write continuously for five minutes, putting down whatever comes to mind.

After five minutes, stop writing and reread what you wrote. Use your freewriting to help you make a case for the robbery being genuine or pretend. Compare your conclusion with those of your classmates.

memories

You may at times remember without intending it, perhaps without even knowing what it means. The melody of a song may suddenly pop into your head. Or, you may think of a person you haven't seen in a long time.

It's easy to let these fleeting memories pass with little thought. But they probably are important. After all, your memories are what make you *you*, make you different from anyone else.

American novelist Thomas Wolfe took such memories seriously. His writing is based on this sort of remembering. He wrote,

> I would be sitting, for example, on the terrace of a café watching the flash and play of life before me on the Avenue de l'Opera and suddenly I would remember the iron railing that goes along the boardwalk at Atlantic City. I could see it instantly just the way it was, the heavy iron pipe; its raw galvanized look; the way the joints were fitted together. It was all so vivid and concrete that I could feel my hand upon it and know the exact dimensions, its size and weight and shape. . . . I would sit there, looking out upon the Avenue de l'Opera and my life would ache with the whole memory of it; the desire to see it again; somehow to find a word for it; a language that would tell its shape, its color, the way we have all known and felt and seen it. And when I understood this thing, I saw that I must find for myself the tongue to utter what I knew but could not say.

As Wolfe describes it, the past has a way of intruding on the present. Some people try to ignore these intrusions. If they suddenly begin to hum a tune, they don't think about what it is or why it came to mind. One reason for such an attitude is that personal memories don't seem like sound thinking. They aren't solid like facts. But does that mean they are not important?

In his novel *Hard Times*, Charles Dickens describes a school devoted to teaching "fact, fact, fact." In one scene, Sissy, a girl whose father trains horses, is asked by Mr. Gradgrind to give her definition of a horse. She is so

surprised by this request that she cannot speak, and Mr. Gradgrind concludes that she knows nothing about horses. He then asks a boy named Bitzer to give his definition. Bitzer replies:

> Quadruped. Graminivorous. Forty teeth, namely, twenty-four
> grinders, four eye-teeth, and twelve incisive. Sheds coat in the spring;
> in marshy countries, sheds hoofs too. Hoofs hard, but requiring to be
> shod with iron. Age known by marks in mouth.

Bitzer's definition pleases Mr. Gradgrind, who says to Sissy, "Now you
know what a horse is."

Readers of *Hard Times* realize, of course, that Sissy knows much more
than Bitzer about horses. The difference is that while Bitzer's knowledge of
horses consists of a dictionary definition, Sissy's is made up of hundreds of
thousands of memories of horses she has seen. Bitzer can easily produce his
knowledge. Sissy must work harder to produce hers. Her problem is like
Thomas Wolfe's: she can remember more than she has words for.

To use reflectively what you remember calls for you to be sensitive, like
Wolfe, to unexpected memories. Try to see how what you remember fits with
what is before your eyes. Bring your past to bear on the present. Reflective
thinking is not the computation of a machine that spits out definitions like
Bitzer's. It is a human being's personal attempt to make sense of things. And
remembering is part of the attempt.

Activity 6.3

Following are three common experiences. Write about each of them, but
don't define them. Don't say what everyone already knows. Probe your
memory. For each experience, write down what you remember. Wring out
your mind. Get as much detail and meaning as you can. When you finish,
look over what you have written. How do you think these memories are still
affecting you? (You may want to save your notes for this activity in your
folder.)

1. a sensation of pain

2. an important conversation

3. a feeling of satisfaction

rethinking

A SUMMARY

Remembering has two aspects—putting things into your memory and pulling them out. You can do both—memorize and recall—more effectively if you use mnemonic strategies. They help you to consciously classify or reconstruct what you are trying to remember. For example, familiar objects can be used to help you remember the items on a list, by attaching something difficult to remember to something that is easy to remember. Questions also help you focus on details so that you can remember them better. Patterns, key facts, and easy-to-remember rules reduce the amount you need to memorize and make recollection easier.

Your memory is more, however, than a filing system. Remembering is often like discovery. Techniques that draw on your memory, like brainstorming, can pull things out of your memory you didn't even know were there.

Remembering is, in fact, the basis of reflective thinking. You—your identity, your way of seeing the world—are made of memories.

To practice reflective remembering, write a narrative of an incident you observed or took part in. You can choose any incident. It might be something, say an accident, that you were only a witness to. Or, it could be something, say a day at a theme park, that you were a part of. It could be a scene you recall from years ago or something that happened last week. It could be something you remember because it was funny, because it made you proud of yourself, or perhaps because it puzzled you. It can be a long story or a short one.

In your narrative, tell not only what happened but also why the incident was important then and is important now. Instead of narrating the events from your own point of view, tell the story as you think someone else might have seen it. In other words, you need to pull out of your memory more than what *you* felt at the time. Think about the others who were involved. Remember the events from their point of view. Choose one of those others to be the narrator of the incident and tell what that person saw and felt.

Hart Day Leavitt

PART TWO

Miró, Joan.
Dutch Interior, I. 1928.
Oil on canvas, 36⅛ × 28¾".
Collection, The Museum of Modern Art, New York.
Mrs. Simon Guggenheim Fund.

IMAGINING

When sixteenth-century French essayist Montaigne wrote about imagination, he noted the power of the mind to make unreal things seem real. If he spent time with someone who was sick, he wrote, his imagination began to make him think he had the illness, too. For Montaigne, the imagination worked on its own, without his control, and the world it created was false.

These two ideas about imagination—that it works unconsciously and that it is just make-believe—are only partly true. Often, creative ideas do come suddenly and at odd moments. An idea may pop into your mind while you're taking a shower. Or, you may be eating and suddenly get an idea from the way the mashed potatoes are lumped on your plate. And everyone has heard the story of Sir Isaac Newton being struck on the head with an apple. It is said that he was also struck with an idea—namely, that the gravity of Earth might pull on the moon just as it pulls on an apple.

Imagination works in such mysterious ways that even people who are creative cannot explain it. That may be exactly the point: being creative or imaginative is thinking in a way that cannot be predicted. This doesn't mean, however, that imagination is all daydreams and make-believe. The power of your imagination to generate new ideas can help you make sense of the real world.

There are many methods you can use to draw on your imagination. The chapters that follow describe eight different ways you can begin imagining.

VII

CREATING POSSIBILITIES

"What if." These are magic words. They add new lands to the realm of possibility. "What if I rub two sticks together?" Some ancient human may have asked that question and discovered fire. A sixteenth-century Italian sailor asked himself what if he sailed west across the unknown Atlantic Ocean. The sailor—Christopher Columbus—discovered the Americas. A sixteen-year-old German schoolboy asked himself what would happen if he could send out a beam of light and keep up with it. The boy was Albert Einstein, and ten years later, his what-if led him to conceive the theory of relativity.

In this chapter, you will try some what-ifs of your own. You won't find new continents, but you may expand your horizons. First, you'll discover the possibilities of wordplay. *What if* you use words in unexpected ways?

Then, you'll create new possibilities with variations on themes. What if you rearrange the parts of something familiar?

You'll also find new possibilities in an old story by changing your sympathies. What if you tell a story from the "bad guy's" point of view?

Finally, you'll play with the possibilities of imaginary history. What if a historical event happened differently? How would that affect the chain of events that came after?

wordplay

> "Take some more tea," the March Hare said to Alice, very earnestly.
>
> "I've had nothing yet," Alice replied in an offended tone, "so I can't take more."
>
> "You mean you can't take *less*," said the Hatter. "It's very easy to take *more* than nothing."
>
> —LEWIS CARROLL

This wordplay (from *Alice's Adventures in Wonderland*) illustrates one way of creating new possibilities. Change the meaning of a word by taking it in one sense rather than another and, suddenly, what seemed familiar becomes new.

A similar effect is created with puns, another of Lewis Carroll's favorite kinds of wordplay. When Alice asks the Mock Turtle what subjects he studied in school, he replies, "Reeling and Writhing, of course, to begin with . . . and then the different branches of Arithmetic—Ambition, Distraction, Uglification, and Derision."

Using words in unexpected ways can make you think as well as laugh. Turning the world on its head puts life in a new perspective.

Activity 7.1

A The following dialogue is from the Marx Brothers movie *Duck Soup*. Groucho Marx has been made President of Freedonia and is conducting a cabinet meeting in his own special way. What sorts of wordplay can you find in this scene?

MINISTER OF LABOR: The Department of Labor wishes to report that the workers of Freedonia are demanding shorter hours.

GROUCHO: Very well, we'll give them shorter hours. We'll start by cutting their lunch hour to twenty minutes. And now, gentlemen, we've got to start looking for a Treasurer.

MINISTER OF LABOR: But you appointed one last week.

GROUCHO: That's the one I'm looking for.

SECRETARY OF WAR: Gentlemen! Gentlemen! Enough of this. How about taking up the tax?

GROUCHO: How about taking up the carpet?

SECRETARY OF WAR: I still insist we must take up the tax.

GROUCHO: He's right. You've got to take up the tacks before you can take up the carpet.

SECRETARY OF WAR: I give all my time and energies to my duties and what do I get?

GROUCHO: You get awfully tiresome after a while.

SECRETARY OF WAR: Sir, you try my patience!

GROUCHO: I don't mind if I do. You must come over and try mine some time.

SECRETARY OF WAR: That's the last straw! I resign! I wash my hands of the whole business!

GROUCHO: A good idea. You can wash your neck, too.

B   Amelia Bedelia is a character in a series of children's books who is known for taking things literally. If someone tells her to draw the draperies, you can bet that she will sit down with a pad of paper and a pencil and sketch them. Or, if she is told to dust the furniture, you know that she will put dust on the sofa and chairs, not wipe it off. That would be *un*dusting the furniture.

Working either on your own or with a group of classmates, make a list of expressions that might be used in one of author Peggy Parrish's Amelia Bedelia books. The expressions should contain words that can be taken more than one way.

If you like, you might even try to write a short story about a character who causes trouble by taking literally the expressions you listed.

C   Think of a playful way to read one of the newspaper headlines that follow. (All of them are actual headlines.) Then write the first paragraph of a news story that would go along with your reading of the headline.

For One Man, Solidarity Is Nothing but Splinters

Fresh Air Fund Youths Get Connecticut Respite

A One-Time Aide to Bush Shows a Lobbyist's Magic

Americas' Indians Tied to Asians

Buzzing National Parks

variations

In music, a common way of creating new possibilities is to vary a theme. Composers start with a tune and then invent variations by changing it in all sorts of ways—speeding it up, slowing it down, shifting the key, adding notes, dropping notes, changing the harmony. A lot of jazz is based on playing variations on a theme.

You don't need a musical theme to invent variations, though. You can start with anything. For instance, many word games challenge players to see how many words they can make from a given group of letters.

The way to find variations is easy, and it is much the same whether you are starting with a group of letters, a melody, or even a mathematical equation. You rearrange the parts of what you began with, looking for new arrangements that make sense. Suppose, for instance, you begin with the equation for finding the circumference of a circle:

$$C = D \bullet \pi$$

(C = circumference; D = diameter; π = about 3.1416; and $\bullet$ = multiply by)

This equation can be varied in these ways:

$$D = C \div \pi \qquad \pi = C \div D$$

Notice that these variations do not change the meaning of the equation. In each case, the three parts are related to each other in the same way. All that has changed is the way in which the information is presented. When you vary a theme, you can't change everything.

Activity 7.2

A Think of groups that you could form from the following numbers: 1, 2, 3, 4, 5, 6, 7, 8, 9, 10, 11, 12. For each group, state the rule that defines the group. You can state the rule in words or as a formula. For example, here is one group:

1, 3, 5, 7, 9, 11

And here are two ways to state the rule that defines the group:

1. All numbers in the group are odd.

2. $n \div 2 \neq x$
    (n = a number in the group; x = a positive integer)

Here is a different group and the rule that defines it.

1, 2

$$n^2 - 2n \leq 0$$

(n = a number in the group; $n^2 = n \bullet n$; $\leq$ = "less than or equal to")

Make a list of the groups you can come up with. You might want to work in a group with three or four classmates.

B   The dots in the illustration that follows are one centimeter apart. By connecting the dots, how many different shapes can you draw that will have an area of two square centimeters? On a sheet of paper, draw the shapes you think of. Compare your drawings with those of your classmates. (Hint: The area of the entire layout is four square centimeters.)
    One solution is shown.

•   •   •   Solution

•   •   •

•   •   •

C   Using all or some of the following, what pictures can you draw?

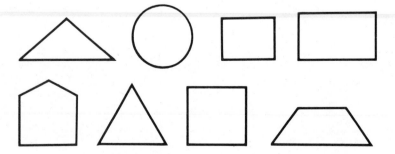

D Each time you speak or write, you choose from scores of possible ways you might express yourself. How many variations can you think of for the following sentence?

> She entered the room.

Write down as long a list of variations as you can. Compare your list with those of your classmates. Here is one variation to get you started:

> On her hands and knees, Elena dragged herself into the kitchen.

E A movie actor was instructed by director William Wyler to enter the room and hang his hat on the hook by the door. The actor asked how Wyler wanted him to play the scene. Wyler was puzzled. How many ways are there to hang up a hat? The actor then demonstrated ten different ways.

Try performing the act of hanging up a hat (or choose some similar ordinary act) for your classmates. See how many genuinely different ways you can play the scene. You might consider varying the speed of your motions, the way you move your body, and your facial expressions.

changing sympathies

The Old English epic poem *Beowulf* is a monster story that is over a thousand years old. It tells of a half-human monster named Grendel who, for twelve years, terrorizes the castle of Hrothgar in Denmark. The young hero Beowulf hears of the monster and decides to help destroy him. With fourteen fellow warriors, he sails from Sweden to Hrothgar's castle, where a feast is given to honor Beowulf. After the feast, the warriors wait to see if Grendel will appear.

Sure enough, that very night Grendel breaks in the door.

> The fiend wasted no time, but for a start snatched up a sleeping man. He tore him apart in an instant, crunched the body, drank blood from its veins, and gulped it down in great bites until he had wholly swallowed the dead man, even the hands and feet.
>
> —trans. DAVID WRIGHT

The warriors try to use their swords to hack at Grendel, but it is no use. The monster has cast a spell that makes him impervious to blades.

Beowulf, meanwhile, has grabbed Grendel's claw, grabbed it and will not let go. The monster struggles in vain to free himself. Finally, Beowulf (who is, the poem says, the strongest man in the world) wrenches the monster's arm off at the shoulder. Grendel is just able to drag himself off to the swamp to die.

American writer John Gardner saw some possibilities in this old tale, and in 1971, Gardner published his novel *Grendel*. As you might imagine, it tells the story from the point of view of the monster. In Gardner's telling, Grendel rages about the stupidity of his twelve-year war, laughs at heroism, and, for a while at least, is pleased to see the fifteen warriors who come from Sweden. He thinks he will have some fun with these new would-be heroes. Then Grendel discovers that Beowulf is clever as well as strong.

In the end, Grendel feels that he has been beaten not by Beowulf's strength or heroism, but by an accident. He tried to kick Beowulf but slipped on the bloody floor. Dying friendless in the swamp, he is surrounded by former enemies who have gathered to watch. It seems to Grendel that they enjoy the sight.

In this retelling of the Beowulf poem, Gardner has shifted the reader's sympathies by focusing on Grendel. He shows the monster to be more than an obstacle for Beowulf to overcome. The reader becomes interested in what Grendel thinks and feels, and, seeing the story in this new way, discovers new possibilities in it.

Activity 7.3

You can do the same sort of thing that Gardner did. Begin by selecting an old, familiar story. Choose one that has a character who is important to the story but is not sympathetic, maybe even the villain. Then retell the story from that character's point of view. You might, for example, choose a fairy tale, say "The Three Little Pigs," and tell the story from the point of view of the wolf. Find out how changing sympathies opens up new possibilities.

imaginary history

About sixty years ago, British statesman and historian Winston Churchill wrote an essay in which he imagined what the world would be like if Lee had won the Battle of Gettysburg and the South had won the Civil War. Writing as though his imaginary history were true, he tells how Great Britain supported the new nation, how slavery was abolished, how the South remained economically strong. He tells, further, how in 1905, Great Britain, the United States, and the Confederate States joined to form the "English-speaking Association." This association, he says, was so influential that in 1914, when the nations of Europe were being drawn toward war, the association maintained the peace by announcing that it would join with any nation that was attacked.

Imagining what might have happened if a historical event had turned out differently is another way of creating new possibilities. Thinking about how things could have been different in the past can be a reminder of how they might be made different for the future.

This sort of imagining doesn't need to begin with an event like the Battle of Gettysburg. British writer Hilaire Belloc began an essay of imaginary history by asking himself what would have happened if a cart had been stuck. The cart he had in mind was the one that was pulled in front of the carriage of King Louis XVI as he tried to escape from France in 1791. Changing this small event, Belloc imagines that the French Revolution would have failed, the balance of power in Europe in the nineteenth century would have been changed, and World War I would never have occurred.

All sorts of possibilities come to mind when you begin to ask, what might have happened if . . . ? British poet and essayist J. C. Squires wrote, in the introduction to a collection of essays of imaginary history, "There is no action or event, great or small . . . which might not have happened differently, and, happening differently, have perhaps modified the world's history for all time. . . . Somebody in Tibet may have a bad night's sleep, or sleep too long, and the fates of nations will be involved."

Activity 7.4

You can create some possibilities with your own imaginary history. Think of an event, great or small, and imagine how it might have happened differently. Phrase the situation as a question, such as, what might have happened if John F. Kennedy had not been assassinated? Write your question at the top of a piece of paper. Beneath it, list subsequent events you think would have been altered by this one event turning out differently. Share your list with your classmates and see if they find your imaginary history believable.

You might also try the same idea with your personal history. Think of how an event in your life might have happened differently. Then list subsequent events that would have been altered. You could share this list with friends or family members to see what they think of this imaginary autobiography.

rethinking

A   SUMMARY

In this chapter you have explored four kinds of what-ifs. You tried wordplay, made some variations on a theme, changed your sympathies, and wrote an imaginary history. All these are ways to create possibilities, ways to come up with new ideas.

Creating possibilities reflectively is more than just mixing things up. Wordplay that makes no sense, for example, is foolish, not funny. Reflective possibilities draw what might be from what is.

To practice creating possibilities, you will try your hand at a kind of fiction that is based on the question What if?—science fiction. To plan your story, think of an invention, such as a machine that generates solid images in three dimensions or a computer that operates from thought impulses. This invention will be your what-if. It doesn't need to be something outlandish or scientifically complicated. It could be as simple as a fertilizer that grows giant vegetables. Or, you could even use an *un*-invention as your what-if—for instance, what if television had never been invented?

Next, think about how your invention (or *un*-invention) would change people's lives. Make a list of possible outcomes for different sorts of people.

Finally, use your notes to write a short story that tells what would happen if . . .

VIII

FINDING RELATIONSHIPS

N o idea can exist by itself. Try to think of only one object and of nothing else—say, a pencil.

Pretty soon, you'll find that you are thinking of its hexagonal shape, or its color, or the way the eraser is worn down. You'll think of the graphite inside the wood, of forests where the wood is harvested, of factories where workers make the pencils. You'll think of messages you've written or might write with a pencil. You'll think of letters and languages and peoples.

In fact, if you think about that pencil long enough, you'll end up thinking about the whole world and all of human history. Each thought is related to others, and they in turn are related. No thought stands alone.

One aspect of imaginative thinking is being aware of relationships. This sometimes requires effort, because the relationships aren't always obvious. The imaginative thinker seeks them out. In this chapter, you will find relationships in four ways. First, you will see how analogies define relationships. Then, you will see how allusions and metaphors evoke unexpected relationships. You'll also see how language itself is a tool for creating relationships. Finally, you'll look at how you are related to others and to the world around you.

analogies

When you say that two things are related, what exactly are you saying about them? For instance, you would probably agree that teachers and chalk are related in some way and that acorns are related to oaks. But are you saying the same thing in each case?

Obviously not. A teacher uses chalk in his or her work. An oak produces acorns and grows from one. The relationships between the items in each pair are quite different.

Suppose, however, that you compared the relationship between *teacher* and *chalk* to the relationship between *carpenter* and *hammer*. Now, the items in each pair are related to one another in the same way. In each case, there is a person and a tool the person uses in his or her work. It does not matter that a hammer is even less like a piece of chalk than an acorn is. What is being compared is not these two items, but the relationship between the pairs— *teacher/chalk* and *carpenter/hammer*.

To compare relationships in this way is to construct an *analogy*. The value of analogies is that they help you see what one thing is like by comparing it with something else. Also, they help to focus thinking because an analogy picks out one particular quality—say, the use of an object or its origin.

Analogies can hamper thinking, however. Once you think of things in terms of one relationship, it can be hard to think of them in terms of any other. You can forget that any pair of items has many possible relationships. Suppose someone said that a teacher's use of chalk is like a bookkeeper's use of a quill pen. In this case, the *teacher/chalk* relationship is no longer simply that between a person and a tool the person uses. The analogy with the bookkeeper and the quill pen suggests that there is something old-fashioned and out-of-date about a teacher using chalk.

Or, suppose that someone said that a teacher and chalk were like an artist and paint. Now the chalk is no longer being thought of as a tool at all (whether old-fashioned or not), but as an artistic medium through which something pleasing is created.

In short, an analogy can be a trap if you think that it sums up all the relationships between two objects. You can, however, open up your thinking if you use analogies imaginatively to help you find and think about relationships.

Activity 8.1

A In standardized tests, like the SAT, analogies are often written like this:

up : down : : fast : slow

This analogy would be read "*Up* is to *down* as *fast* is to *slow*."

Here are some analogies in which one item is missing. Fill in the missing item on a separate sheet of paper.

1. clock : time : : scale : _____

2. January : months of the year : : _____ : days of the week

3. bird : flying : : fish : _____

4. heart : blood : : gasoline pump : _____

5. Earth : sun : : moon : _____

B Now that you have had a little practice with analogies, try looking for the analogy in the following passage from *Through the Looking Glass* by Lewis Carroll. When you find it, explain what's wrong with it. See if your classmates agree with your reasoning.

"Would you—be good enough," Alice panted out, after running a little further, "to stop a minute just to get one's breath again?"

"I'm *good* enough," the King said, "only I'm not strong enough. You see, a minute goes by so fearfully quick. You might as well try to stop a Bandersnatch!"

If you have trouble phrasing the analogy, try putting it into this form:

stop : _____ : : stop : _____

C Here are some pairs that could be used as the first part of an analogy. For each pair, list at least three ways to complete the analogy on a separate sheet of paper.

1. child : adult : : _____ : _____

2. car : driver : : _____ : _____

3. football : quarterback : : _____ : _____

4. bath : dog : : _____ : _____

5. rock : music : : _____ : _____

allusions and metaphors

Every day you create relationships. You do it by using language.

> Now is the winter of our discontent
> Made glorious summer by this sun of York;
> And all the clouds that lour'd upon our house
> In the deep bosom of the ocean buried.

Here Shakespeare, in the opening lines of the play *Richard III*, describes a change in the spirit of the times by drawing on the change of seasons. A relationship is created between winter and discontent that gives depth to the mood expressed.

You may say, of course, that Shakespeare was a playwright and poet who lived four hundred years ago—and that real people don't talk that way now. And it is true that English has changed since the time of Shakespeare. But using metaphors—the way that Shakespeare used *winter*—is something that real people do every day.

Recently a transit official in Los Angeles was commenting on the first 19 miles of a proposed 150-mile commuter rail line. He said, "I see this line as a candle in the darkness of our transportation nightmare out here."

In one sentence, he used three words metaphorically—*candle, darkness,* and *nightmare.* He is talking about how the first stretch of rail line is going to alleviate the annoying Los Angeles traffic jams. By relating the 19-mile line to a candle in the darkness, he is emphasizing that it is going to help only a little bit. By relating traffic congestion to a nightmare, he is showing how crowded he believes the highways are.

Metaphors work by bringing the ideas connected with one word—say, *winter* or *candle*— into a relationship with those of another word. Readers see the subject—discontent or commuter rail lines—in a new way because of the influence of the metaphoric words and the ideas connected with them.

Allusions work in much the same way. An allusion is a reference to something well known—a book, a poem, a person, a historical event, a piece of music. The reference draws on the ideas connected with whatever is being alluded to and relates them to the main subject. For instance, at a time when people were more familiar with Shakespeare's plays, a person might say, "Lay on, Macduff," and know that listeners would recognize the allusion to *Macbeth*. Macbeth uses these words to begin his last, desperate combat with Macduff—a fight to the death.

Nowadays, a person might communicate a similar idea with a different allusion: "Go ahead—make my day." These words conjure up the image of the movie character Dirty Harry and his attitude toward criminals. Like "Lay on, Macduff," the line suggests grim determination.

An allusion, like a metaphor, has the power to evoke images and feelings and to create relationships. Using language in these ways, you can express yourself as well as generate new ideas.

Activity 8.2

A Everyday speech is littered with dead metaphors—the leg of a chair, the mouth of a river. These are expressions so common that they no longer sound metaphoric—like the transit official's "candle in the darkness." Listen to the conversations around you for a day and make a list of the dead metaphors you hear. For each one, try to think of a live metaphor that would both express the idea and evoke new relationships.

B A trader leaving the New York Stock Exchange after a hectic day was asked by a reporter how trading had gone. He replied, "Did you see the movie *Animal House*?" What does this allusion tell you about that day's trading? Working with three or four classmates, write an answer to the reporter's question that expresses the same idea, but without the allusion. Discuss which communicates more effectively—the straightforward answer or the allusion.

C Creating metaphors is as much a habit as a skill. To get into the habit, devote a section of your notebook to metaphors. They might be ones you read or hear, or ones you make up yourself. A good place to find metaphors is in the sports pages of a newspaper. A good way to make them up is to ask yourself, when you are describing something, "What does this remind me of?" For instance, a little brother who insists on following you everywhere might remind you of a clinging vine that covers a wall. If you explore relationships, you'll find the seeds of metaphors.

ordinary language

Metaphors and allusions are two ways that you use language to create relationships, but they are only the most obvious ways. They stand out because they are colorful. They enrich your speech and writing with unexpected relationships.

But the very act of using words is itself a matter of creating relationships. Each time you pull a group of words into a sentence, you are saying something that maybe was never said before. Even if the idea your words express is an old one, it may be a new one for you.

To see the power of words to create relationships, read this list:

> people in masks
> dressed in white
> wearing gloves
> sewing shut

By now you are probably imagining doctors and nurses in an operating room. But change a few words in the list, and the relationships are altered. A new scene comes into view.

> people in masks
> dressed in black
> wearing gloves
> alarms sounding

Words act on one another like steel on flint: they strike sparks. Bring a few together, and they conjure up something that didn't exist before.

Activity 8.3

Here's a way you can create some new relationships with ordinary language. Make a list of ten random words. You can do this by simply running your finger down the left-hand column of a dictionary page until you find a familiar word. Flip to a new page and repeat the procedure. You might come up with a list like this:

hare

ultrashort

designated hitter

never

runless

quack

consult

goofy

plethora

tail

Now write something that uses all the words you have listed. It could be a paragraph in the style of a news report, a story, a bit of dialogue—whatever works with the material you have. Just make sure that you *use* the words, not just mention them. The first sentence that follows uses the word *hare*. The second sentence only mentions it.

1. A hare, gnawing on a carrot, slid into second base.

2. *Hare* is another word for *rabbit*.

Let the words guide what you write. With this list, for example, you would probably write something about a baseball game in order to use *designated hitter* and *runless*, but it would probably be a rather *goofy* game.

you and the world

When you think of how you are related to those around you, the first relationships that come to mind are probably those of the family. You have kin. You are a daughter or a son, a sister or a brother, a cousin, a grandchild, a branch in a family tree.

But even if you had no relatives you knew of, even if you were alone in the world, you wouldn't be unrelated. The fact that you can read these words makes you a member of the family of English-speaking people. As a student you have a relationship with those who attend your school and with those who work there. The music you enjoy is enjoyed by others. Your relationships with your fellow human beings are marked by the foods you think are tasty, the clothes you think are fashionable, the jokes you think are funny.

Nineteenth-century American essayist Ralph Waldo Emerson saw in these sorts of relationships a basic component of imaginative thinking. He felt that people depend on their relationships in order to understand what they read.

> We, as we read, must become Greeks, Romans, Turks, priest and
> king, martyr and executioner; must fasten these images to some real-
> ity in our secret experience, or we shall learn nothing rightly.

This sort of sympathy is possible, Emerson thought, because each person is related not only to a few others, but to all people. You have within
yourself the sum of human history.

> All that Shakespeare says of the king, yonder slip of a boy that
> reads in the corner feels to be true of himself. We sympathize in the
> great moments of history, in the great discoveries, the great resis-
> tances, the great prosperities of men;—because there law was en-
> acted, the sea was searched, the land was found, or the blow was
> struck, *for us*, as we ourselves in that place would have done or ap-
> plauded.

Perhaps you have never read yourself into history. But chances are you
have watched characters in movies or on television and sensed that they felt
as you have felt and acted as you would have acted, that they were, in short,
related to you. Your relationships with others are the basis of sympathy and
one of the keys to imaginative thinking.

Activity 8.4

A You can make a map of significant relationships in your life. In the middle of
a sheet of paper, put your name. Then begin thinking of the important people in your life. As you think of them, write their names on the paper. Clus-
ter together those names that belong together. You might connect the
names with lines to show the relationships more clearly.

B To explore the idea of seeing yourself in others, think of one person to whom
you have no obvious relationship. It might be a historical person or perhaps
a character in literature, movies, or on television. List ways that this person
is like you. Think of qualities or actions that show how the two of you are
related.

    Be imaginative in your search for relationships. You might, for in-
stance, take the character Bugs Bunny and find that he, like you, lives by his
wits, enjoys carrots, and has big feet.

    When you complete your list, share it with a few people who know you
well. See what they think of the relationships you have discovered.

rethinking

A SUMMARY

You've seen in this chapter how finding relationships promotes imaginative thinking. For example, by helping you focus on and define relationships, analogies help you find connections. Metaphors and allusions evoke new ideas by creating unexpected relationships. And ordinary language creates relationships by the simple act of bringing words together. You yourself are a network of relationships, as you are touched by everyone and everything around you.

To practice thinking imaginatively about relationships, write a character sketch in which you describe a person by showing how he or she relates to others. This technique is often used by novelists and short-story writers. Here is how Washington Irving describes Rip Van Winkle:

> Certain it is, that he was a great favorite among all the good wives of the village, who, as usual with the amiable sex, took his part in all family squabbles. . . . The children of the village, too, would shout with joy whenever he approached. He assisted at their sports, made their playthings, taught them to fly kites and shoot marbles, and told them long stories of ghosts, witches and Indians. Whenever he went dodging about the village, he was surrounded by a troop of them hanging on his skirts, clambering on his back, and playing a thousand tricks on him with impunity; and not a dog would bark at him throughout the neighborhood.

The character you describe should be a person you invent, someone your readers know nothing about. Portray the character by showing how others react to or feel about him or her. Some of the relationships can be negative; they don't all have to be positive like Rip Van Winkle's. Bring the character to life by putting him or her in the center of a web of relationships.

IX

SEEING PATTERNS

When you see a pattern for a dress, you know what it is. You recognize it as the model someone would use to cut material to sew a dress. Its function is obvious.

Suppose, however, that you see only the finished dress. Can you visualize the pattern from which it came? Could you see in the dress the pattern that was used to make it?

All around you are patterns, but most of them, like the pattern for the dress, do not announce themselves. To see the pattern, you have to look beyond the facts. Scientist and essayist Stephen Jay Gould says it this way:

> My talent is making connections. That's why I am an essayist. . . . Can you see a pattern? I'm always trying to see a pattern in this forest and I'm tickled that I can do that. . . . I can sit down on just about any subject and think of about twenty things that relate to it and they're not hokey connections. They're real connections that you can forge into essays or scientific papers. . . . It took me years to realize that was a skill. I could never understand why everbody just didn't *do* that. . . . Most people *don't* do it. They just don't see the connections.

In this chapter you will practice the skill of seeing patterns. You'll look first at sequences. Then, you'll look at causes and effects. Finally, you'll see how stories combine both.

sequence

The simplest kind of pattern is a sequence. Anytime you put things into an order, you are creating a sequence. It might run from the first to last, like the letters of the alphabet. It might run from north to south, like numbered streets. A sequence can be ordered from most to least, as, for example, when people line up according to height. The steps in a process are a sequence. A recipe, the instructions for putting a bicycle together, the procedure airline pilots follow before takeoff—each of these has a pattern, because it follows a predictable sequence.

Recognizing the pattern behind a sequence calls for more than knowing what comes next. To see the pattern, you have to understand how things are organized. Suppose, for example, that you live on 51st Street and you know that 54th Street is three blocks south of where you live. Does this mean that you understand how the streets are arranged?

Not necessarily. If someone asks you where 47th Street is and you have no idea, then you do not understand the pattern. All that you have done is memorize where some of the streets are. It's possible to memorize parts of a sequence without really understanding the pattern behind it, just as a parrot can repeat words without understanding them.

To uncover patterns, you need to be on the lookout for them. When you see a sequence, ask yourself why it's ordered this way instead of another. And don't be discouraged if the pattern isn't obvious. Usually, there is a reason for how things are organized, even if they look disorganized. A desk that looks like a chaotic mess of books and papers may, for the person who works there, be organized in a perfectly sensible pattern.

Activity 9.1

A Briefly explain the pattern behind each of the following sequences.

1. 1, 1, 2, 4, 8, 16, 32, 64 . . .

2. airplane, car, horse, bicycle, feet

3. airplane, bicycle, car, feet, horse

4. Alexander the Great, Julius Caesar, Genghis Kahn, Napoleon Bonaparte, Adolf Hitler

5. vernal equinox, summer solstice, autumnal equinox, winter solstice

6. San Francisco, Denver, St. Louis, Philadelphia

7. couplet, sonnet, essay, novel

8. Washington, Jefferson, Lincoln, Hamilton, Jackson, Grant, Franklin

9. triangle, square, pentagon, hexagon . . .

10. melting point of ice, normal body temperature, boiling point of water, melting point of gold

B The following sentences are listed in alphabetical order, according to the first word in each. Arrange them according to a different pattern. Share and discuss your pattern with your classmates.

1. A little farther down the road, she met two little girls.

2. Along the way, she met an old man with a sad story.

3. He said that his wife was sick, but he had no money to pay a doctor.

4. Immediately, she tied one end of the rope to a tree and threw the other to the young man.

5. In a sack she carried a gold coin, a loaf of bread, and a length of rope.

6. Later, as she rested near a river, she heard someone calling for help.

7. Once upon a time, a young princess went out in disguise to visit the kingdom.

8. She looked up and saw a young man caught in the river's current.

9. She was dressed in the ordinary clothes of a commoner.

10. So the princess gave him the coin.

11. So the princess gave them the loaf of bread.

12. They said they were alone in the world and were very hungry.

cause and effect

Suppose you are the kind of person who likes to keep track of things. You record the length of your shadow in sunlight. You stand in the same place and measure your shadow in the morning, at noon, and in the late afternoon, and you find that it is longer early and late in the day than in the middle of the day. You continue keeping your records for a whole year. Even though you measure it at the same times each day, the length of the shadow changes from one day to the next. It is longest in the middle of winter. Day by day, it gets shorter until, in the middle of summer, it is at its shortest. In fact, at noon in the middle of summer, the shadow is so short there is not enough to measure. After that, day by day it begins to grow longer again.

What do you make of this pattern of events? To begin with, you might notice that you are dealing with a cause and an effect. The sun is the cause, and the length of your shadow is the effect. By blocking the sun's light, you cast the shadow. But what causes the pattern of change?

To think about this, it helps to see that you actually have two different patterns that are similar to one another. First, there is the changing length of your shadow during the day, and, second, there is the changing length of your shadow each day over the course of a year. In each of these patterns, three different things are related. In the first, the sun, the length of your shadow, and the time of day are somehow connected. In the second pattern, the sun and the length of your shadow are connected with the seasons.

When you think about the first pattern this way, it isn't too difficult to understand. The sun begins and ends the day low in the sky. At these times, its light strikes you at a low angle, and this low angle casts a long shadow. At noon, the angle of the sun's light is steeper, and the shadow is shorter. The length of the shadow changes with the position of the sun in the sky. That's the pattern.

But what of the second pattern? How do the seasons of the year relate to the changing length of your shadow?

One possibility is that the pattern isn't connected to the seasons at all. Over the course of a year, your height may change, and your growth would affect the shadow's length. But this explanation doesn't fit the facts, because if the day-to-day change in the length of the shadow was caused by your growing taller, then the shadow wouldn't get shorter in the summer.

No, the facts show that the second pattern must be like the first. The length of the shadow is altered by the position of the sun in the sky. In summer, when the shadow is short, the sun must be high in the sky. In winter, when the shadow is long, the sun must be low in the sky.

Now it may be that all this talk about shadows and the sun was obvious to you. It must seem like a long way to go just to prove that having summer means that your part of the world is tilted toward the sun. After all, you already knew that. But the point was not to prove anything about seasons, shadows, and the sun. The point was to show how patterns of cause and effect are a part of everyday life. They are one of the ordinary ways to make sense of the facts you encounter.

Being aware of and looking for patterns of cause and effect can help you think more imaginatively. Patterns show how things that may not, at first glance, seem related (like seasons, shadows, and the sun) really are connected with one another.

Activity 9.2

Most of the time, seeing patterns is harder than it was with the sun and your shadow, because usually there are many facts to consider, and it isn't clear how they relate to one another. The following data provide an example. These are facts that might have been collected about four high school teachers and their students. Look over the facts for connections. What patterns can you find? Why do some of these students do better (their achievement percentile is higher) than others?

	Teachers			
	A	B	C	D
IQ	103	122	99	107
Strictness	4[a]	3	4	2
Hair color	black	blond	gray	gray
Shoe size	11	7	10	8
Students' aptitude percentile	54	48	47	53
Students' achievement percentile	56	50	59	64

[a]0 = not strict,
5 = very strict

Together with three or four classmates, discuss the facts and write down the cause-effect pattern that you think explains the students' achievement results. Compare your conclusion with those of other groups.

stories

Beginning, middle, end—the pattern of a story is familiar to people of all ages all around the world. Even little children know what to expect when they hear the words "Once upon a time. . . ." If a friend walks up to you with a grin on her face and asks, "Have you heard the one about . . . ?" you know what to expect—a story, and probably a funny one.

Stories are one way of putting experiences into patterns. They organize events by arranging them in chronological order. But more than that, stories offer explanations. By arranging events, stories show how the events are connected. In fact, people often tell a story in order to answer the question, "Why did that happen?"

Suppose a friend is to meet you at the mall at four o'clock, but she doesn't show up until five. You ask her, "Why are you late?"

She launches into a scientific explanation of how watches work and what happens when their power source is depleted. At first, you're confused, but finally you figure out that she's telling you that her watch stopped, so she didn't know what time it was.

What's wrong with your friend's explanation? The facts she tells you *do* answer the question you asked. And she puts them into a pattern that makes sense. An explanation of how watches work is a perfectly good cause-effect pattern. It is a scientific explanation.

However, it's the wrong pattern. What you wanted was a historical explanation. You wanted a story. You wanted to know how what she was doing led to her showing up an hour late.

Of course, stories are used for more than explaining a person's actions. They are used to explain why the English colonies in America revolted in 1776, and why Ivan the Terrible was a bad czar, and why the dust bowl of the 1930s caused a lot of people to move to California.

Activity 9.3

Stories can even be used to create a pattern for events that don't involve people. Read through the facts that follow, looking for a pattern. The facts are related to the extinction of the dinosaurs 65 million years ago. Use the facts to write a story that offers one possible explanation for why the dinosaurs disappeared. When you finish your story, share it with your classmates.

1. Scientists have found that layers of rock older than 65 million years contain fossils of tiny organisms.

2. In the layer of rock 65 million years old—a layer called the K/T boundary—the fossils no longer appear.

3. The K/T boundary contains an unusually high level of a rare element called irridium.

4. Most of the irridium on Earth has come from meteorites.

5. A meteorite that is large enough could, when it struck Earth, cause a dust cloud that would encircle the globe and alter the climate by lowering temperatures around the world.

rethinking

A SUMMARY

Patterns help you think more imaginatively by giving you ways of organizing the facts and events you encounter. To see a pattern is to see connections between things that are not obviously connected. To see a pattern is to begin to understand why things are the way they are.

The most basic kind of pattern is a sequence, a way of lining things up. A second kind of pattern is cause and effect. To see a cause-effect pattern is to recognize that one situation or event brings about a second situation or event. The third kind of pattern you looked at in this chapter was the pattern of a story. Stories combine the chronology of a sequence and the explanation of cause and effect. Telling stories is one way that you share the patterns that you see in the world.

To practice thinking imaginatively about patterns, write an essay that explains a process. The process you choose can be a natural one, such as how volcanoes erupt, or it can be a process of production or manufacture, such as how to build a kite or even fold a paper airplane. You should choose a process that you either know something about or are interested in learning about.

In your essay, get behind the facts. You might include diagrams with your essay. However you explain it, make the process so clear that even someone who knows nothing about the subject can understand how the process works. Think about the connections involved and help your readers see the pattern.

X

MAKING MEANING

French mathematician and physicist Jules-Henri Poincaré was puzzled by the inability of some people to understand mathematics. He said that although he didn't expect everyone to discover mathematical proofs and theorems, he was surprised that people couldn't understand a mathematical argument as soon as it was stated. Why, he wondered, did people have to spend time going over something that was already worked out? Why didn't they just see it?

An answer to this question was offered by Mary Henle, a social scientist. She said that what Poincaré didn't realize was that understanding is a creative act. To understand the solution to a problem is like working out the problem for yourself. You can't know what the solution means until you think it through, step by step.

Henle was pointing out that meaning isn't something you can find lying around. You don't see it the way you see the color of the sky. You have to make meaning. Understanding is an act of the imagination.

In this chapter, you'll look at three ways that you make meaning. The first way is by naming things. The second is by getting inside ideas to see their structure. The third is by putting ideas into your own words.

names

To give something a name is to define it, to put it in its place. Names have power. That's why children call one another bad names when they get angry. And it's why many groups of people—from the ancient Hebrews to the

Dobuans of Dobu Island near New Guinea—kept secret the name of their god or gods. They believed that to know the name was to have the power of command. For the same reason, it was common among many native American tribes to have two names—one public, one private. The belief that names have power also appears in folktales. When the queen guesses the name of Rumpelstiltskin, she has power over him.

Names have a lot to do with thinking because they affect how you see the world. Ask yourself this: how many different colors can you recognize?

Chances are that the number you guess will be rather small, because you haven't very many names for colors. For instance, if you look at the grass in the park or the leaves on a maple tree or the bottom light on a traffic signal, you probably see green. But if you look closely, those greens really aren't the same. In fact, if you needed to, you could learn to distinguish— perhaps even to name—thousands of different colors. You see them every day, and yet, in a sense, you don't see them at all, because you don't have names for them.

Because names affect how people see the world, they also affect how people feel about issues. National surveys show that most people are against spending more tax money on "welfare." At the same time, most people are in favor of "helping out the poor." The word *welfare* has bad connotations for many people.

Other words—other names—have good connotations. Suppose, for example, that you read an article in a scientific magazine. Would you trust what it said?

If you answer yes, your reason is probably that "science" is reliable and trustworthy. "Science" shows people how the world works. If something is "scientific," it ought to be believed.

Even if you don't agree with these connotations for *science*, you know many people do. For them, to give something the name *science* is to praise it.

Naming is one way that you make meaning in the world. And if you reflect about how you use this power, you may be surprised at how you can imaginatively make new meanings.

Activity 10.1

A Here are two riddles made up by Lewis Carroll:

> Which is better—a clock that is right once in two years or a clock that is right twice a day?

Which is better—a clock that loses a minute a day or one that doesn't run?

After you have answered each riddle for yourself, try them out on some other people and see what answers you get. You will probably find that people tend to give the same answers. Most will choose the clock that is right twice a day and the clock that loses a minute a day.

See how many people notice that Carroll makes one clock sound better than the other by the way he names them. You see, both questions are about the same two clocks: A clock that loses a minute each day is right once in two years, and a clock that doesn't run at all is right twice a day. Whether one clock sounds better than the other depends on how it is named.

B On June 21, 1990, the U.S. House of Representatives voted on whether to propose a constitutional amendment that would ban desecration of the flag. The next day two newspapers reported the outcome of the vote in articles with these headlines:

House Kills Flag Amendment

Flag Amendment Fails in House

What do you think each paper's editorial policy was on the amendment? How can you tell? (Hint: What words do the papers use to describe what happened? Who or what is named as the actor in each headline?) Discuss your conclusions and your reasons with your classmates.

C Writers of fiction often try to reveal something about their characters through the character's name. In an allegory like John Bunyon's *Pilgrim's Progress*, the names show that the characters stand for qualities—Mr. Legality, Mr. Good-will, and Mr. Worldly Wiseman. In the novels of Charles Dickens, the names are both revealing and humorous. A character who is shallow and superficial is called "Veneering," named for the thin layer of finer wood that is used to cover cheap wood. In another novel a narrow-minded teacher who stifles the curiosity of his students is called "Mc-Choakumchild."

This use of names in fiction has been applied to places as well as people. When nineteenth-century novelist Samuel Butler wrote about a newly discovered and fantastic country, he called the place Erewhon. This name was created by rearranging the letters of the word *nowhere*.

Make a list of names—fantastic, strange, or humorous. Then, for each one, describe some people or places the name might refer to. Suppose, for instance, that you start with the name "Pasta Fortissimo." Is it the name of

- a town with the world's largest spaghetti factory?
- an entree made with giant linguini?
- the world's greatest and fattest Italian tenor?
- a rock band from Italy?

getting inside

C = n y = = r = = d th = s s = nt = nc = ?

Chances are you *can* read that sentence. And though you may not be surprised at your ability to figure out an incomplete message, this ability really is amazing.

If your mind worked the way a computer does, the problem would be much more complicated, and the solution would not be amazing at all. It would simply be trial-and-error. You would go through the alphabet, trying each letter in each blank and discarding the possibilities that make no sense, such as this one:

Cqn ytk rofd thss shntnncd?

Eventually you would reach the likeliest possibility:

Can you read this sentence?

In other words, you would figure out what letters are missing, and then you would read the sentence.

In fact, though, what probably happened is that you read the sentence *before* you knew what the missing letters were. You knew which letters were missing because you knew what the sentence said.

There is nothing magical about this. Most of the time when you read, you don't read every letter or even every word, any more than you pay attention to how the letters are shaped or to how many characters there are in a line of print. Instead, you focus on the ideas that the words are supposed to convey. It's by getting into the ideas that you are able to read anything.

Getting into the ideas, getting inside, is the difference between blindly following a rule and actually seeing the meaning, between a computer and a human mind. Take, for example, this mathematical formula:

$$(n + 1) \times \left(\tfrac{n}{2}\right)$$

This is the formula used to figure out the sum of a series of numbers, such as $1 + 2 + 3 + 4 + 5$. The advantage of using the formula over adding up the numbers is that the formula can be used for a series of any length. The letter n in the formula simply replaces the last number in the series. It would take a long time to add the numbers from 1 to 100, but with the formula, the problem is easily solved:

$$(100 + 1) \times \left(\tfrac{100}{2}\right), \text{ or}$$
$$101 \times 50, \text{ or}$$
$$5050$$

But why does this formula work? What does it really mean?

When you get inside the formula, you see that there are two parts. The first part $(n + 1)$ stands for the pairs that can be made—$100 + 1, 99 + 2, 98 + 3$, and so on.

The second part of the formula $\left(\tfrac{n}{2}\right)$ stands for the number of pairs. There are half as many pairs as there are members in the series.

In other words, the sum of each of the pairs multiplied by the number of pairs gives you the sum of the whole series. And that is what the formula means. To see the meaning, you have to get inside the formula. You have to focus on the idea instead of on the rule.

Activity 10.2

A In both parts of the formula, the value of n is the same. But the meaning of n is different in each part. In the first part $(n + 1)$, what does the n stand for? In the second part $\left(\tfrac{n}{2}\right)$, what does the n stand for?

B The ease with which you can get inside a piece of writing depends more than you might think on the rules of capitalization and punctuation. The following passage—in which nothing has been capitalized and no punctuation marks used—shows just how much meaning lies within these rules. The passage is from Stephen Crane's short story "The Open Boat," which tells what happens to a group of survivors of a shipwreck. Copy the passage and restore the meaning by using capitalization and punctuation.

see it said the captain no said the correspondent slowly i didn't see anything look again said the captain he pointed its exactly in that direction
at the top of another wave the correspondent did as he was bid and this
time his eyes chanced on a small thing on the edge of the swaying horizon it was precisely like the point of a pin it took an anxious eye to find
a lighthouse so tiny think well make it captain if this wind holds and the
boat dont swamp we cant do much else said the captain

in other words

Dictionaries make a word look very solid. Consult a dictionary to learn, for
example, what *honorable* means, and you'll find something like this: "worthy
of respect, of high standing, possessing great integrity." There seems to be no
question about what you should think when you see the word *honorable*. But
then what do you think Antony is trying to say in his famous funeral speech
in Shakespeare's *Julius Caesar*? Antony was Caesar's friend and an enemy of
Brutus and the others who killed Caesar, yet he calls Brutus "honorable."
What does he mean?

> The noble Brutus
> Hath told you Caesar was ambitious;
> If it were so, it was a grievous fault,
> And grievously hath Caesar answered it.
> Here, under leave of Brutus and the rest—
> For Brutus is an honorable man,
> So are they all, all honorable men—
> Come I to speak in Caesar's funeral.
> He was my friend, faithful and just to me,
> But Brutus says he was ambitious,
> And Brutus is an honorable man. . . .
> But yesterday the word of Caesar might
> Have stood against the world; now lies he there,
> And none so poor to do him reverence.
> O masters, if I were disposed to stir
> Your hearts and minds to mutiny and rage,
> I should do Brutus wrong and Cassius wrong,
> Who (you all know) are honorable men.

I will not do them wrong; I rather choose
To wrong the dead, to wrong myself and you,
Than I will wrong such honorable men.

Obviously, there is more in the word *honorable* than one can find in a dictionary. When you hear Antony say the word again and again, you should imagine that he spits it out like a piece of food gone bad. He uses the word not to praise Brutus and his fellows, but to condemn them.

To arrive at the meaning of a piece of writing, you can't treat the sentences as so many equations and the words as fixed quantities. Instead, you have to put yourself into the situation. To understand Antony's funeral oration, for instance, you have to recall that he is picking up the word *honor* from Brutus, who used the word to describe himself. And you also have to see that Antony is trying to sway the mob's feelings gradually. He doesn't dare to say anything against Brutus at the beginning. He wants the mob to decide for themselves that what Brutus has done is wrong.

You make meaning this way whenever you listen and read. You put into your own words the ideas of those who are speaking or writing. Of course, this isn't to say that you can have words mean whatever you choose. Some interpretations are wrong. But without putting ideas into your own words, there is no meaning at all.

Activity 10.3

A One of the fables of La Fontaine tells of a fox and a crow. The crow, on a branch high above the ground, had a piece of cheese in its beak. The fox wanted the cheese for itself, but didn't know how to get it. So the fox began to flatter the crow, telling it how beautiful its voice was and asking it to sing. The crow, which had an ugly voice like all crows do, at first paid no attention. But after a while, the crow began to feel proud of its voice, and it opened its beak to sing. With this, the cheese fell to the ground, and the fox grabbed it and ran off.

Write a moral that you think this fable illustrates. Share your moral with classmates to see if they found a different meaning in the fable.

B Cut out a newspaper article that you think tells an interesting story. Rewrite the story in an entirely different form. For instance, you might turn the material into a poem, a short story, a song, or a play. Share both the original article and your new version with your classmates. See if they think you have preserved the meaning of the original in your version.

C It is not just words that have meaning. Deeds, ways of behaving, even appearance can be meaningful. In the 1960s, long hair on a man or boy suggested that he was probably liberal in his political views. But in the 1790s, it was short hair on a man or boy that meant liberal politics. During much of the twentieth century, a suntan has been a sign of good health and leisure time: people get a tan from lying on the beach. In the nineteenth century, however, only outdoor laborers were tanned. Women especially made every effort to keep their skin as white as possible.

Choose a current fashion that is meaningful. Write a paragraph or more that describes the fashion and explains its meaning. If you know that the fashion had a different meaning at another time or in another country, explain that other meaning, also.

rethinking
A SUMMARY

In this chapter you've seen how making meaning is an imaginative act. You do it by naming and labeling. You shape and color the world by the names you give to things.

You also make meaning by getting inside, by looking past rules to understand the ideas behind them.

And you make meaning by putting ideas into your own words, by putting yourself into your thinking.

To practice making meaning imaginatively, write an essay of definition. Your subject will be the informal social structure among the students at your school. If it's like most schools, there are three or four groups into which most of the students fit. In your essay describe these groups and give the name people use to refer to each group. There may be more than one name for a group. People who belong to the group may call themselves something different from the name used by outsiders. Explain what each name tells about the members of the group and about how the different groups think of and act toward each other.

XI

PREDICTING

In a scene from the movie *The Wizard of Oz*, Dorothy, who is running away from home, meets an old man who offers to tell her fortune. He takes her into his wagon and sits her down before his crystal ball. Then, while she closes her eyes, he looks for clues to her background in the basket she carries and discovers a picture of a farmhouse with a white fence and a woman in a polka-dot dress.

He has Dorothy open her eyes, and he stares intently into his crystal ball, pretending to see her story there. He guesses, eventually, that Dorothy is running away and tells her that he sees a woman in a polka-dot dress standing in front of a farmhouse with a white fence. He says that the woman is crying.

Now, although this fortune-teller cannot see anything in his crystal ball, he really has done a good job of predicting. He assumes that Dorothy's picture shows someone she cares about and that that someone cares about Dorothy also. He predicts that Dorothy's running away will bring worry and unhappiness to the woman in the picture, and this is a sensible prediction. It's not magical, and it doesn't require a crystal ball, but it's an example of how people really can look into the future.

In this chapter, you'll find four ways of predicting. The first is by using natural laws or rules. The second is by figuring out how likely it is that something will happen. The third and fourth ways rely on the use of facts and experience to make reasonable guesses. One kind of guess makes predictions about events that might happen. The other kind makes predictions about events that have already happened.

consequences

"I can foretell the future." If someone said that, you'd be suspicious. But before you cry "Fraud!" think about the times when you have done exactly that. *You* have predicted the future.

Have you ever put water into an ice tray and then placed the tray in a freezer? When you did that, you probably expected that the water would change to ice. And didn't your prediction come true?

And haven't you turned on the television, expecting to see a specific program, and found exactly what you expected?

And certainly you have thrown a ball into the air, expecting it would fall back to Earth, not fly into space. Sure enough, that prediction, too, came true.

Once you begin to notice how easily you are able to predict the future, the ability doesn't seem so remarkable. Many everyday events are governed by well-known patterns and natural laws. Even a three-year-old child can predict the consequences of, say, dropping a glass of milk onto the kitchen floor.

In fact, you may begin to wonder why you aren't able to predict even more. One reason is that few events are completely governed by rules as certain as the law of gravity. Another reason is that you are not always sure what rules or laws apply. Suppose, or example, that a friend is planning to heat a hamburger in a microwave oven. She says that to speed up the process she will put the hamburger into a plastic sandwich bag and close the bag with a twist-tie. What consequences should the two of you be able to predict?

One likely outcome, of course, is that your friend is about to start a fire. As the two of you probably know, metal can burst into flame in a microwave oven. You probably also know (if you think about it) that a twist-tie has a metal wire in it. But you won't be able to predict the consequences of your friend's action unless you recognize that these facts apply.

In short, the ability to predict consequences depends on analyzing a situation to see what facts, rules, or laws are involved. Given the right information, anyone can predict the future.

Activity 11.1

You can demonstrate your own powers of prediction. What comes next in each of the following sequences?

1. Washington, Adams, Jefferson, Madison, . . .

2. 1, 4, 7, 10, . . .

3.

4.

5. run, ran, run; stop, stopped, stopped; swim, swam, swum; wiggle, . . .

6. sunshine, rain, fog, sunshine, snow, clouds, sunshine, fog, clouds, . . .

7. 1:45 P.M., 4:45 P.M., 7:45 P.M., 10:45 P.M., . . .

8. January 1, January 21, February 10, March 2, . . .

9. 1, 4, 2, 5, 3, 6, 4, . . .

10. Venus, Earth, Mars, . . .

chances are

Suppose there are thirty students in your class. What are the chances that two of them have the same birthday?

To guess about something like this is to make a kind of prediction. But it isn't a prediction based on a rule or a natural law. It's a prediction based on a probability. Without knowing all the birthdays, you can't say for certain whether two of them are the same. But you can predict whether that is likely.

Figuring the probability of an event may sound complicated, but it isn't always so. For example, you wouldn't have any trouble predicting the chances of heads coming up if you flip a coin. The chances are fifty-fifty, one out of two. This means that there are two possible outcomes, and "heads" is one of them.

Probabilities are figured the same way. You compare the number of ways in which an event can happen (that's *1* if you're talking about heads coming up) to the number of ways in which that event can both happen and not happen (that's 2 if you're talking about flipping a coin). The resulting ratio ($\frac{1}{2}$) is the probability.

When you say that something is remarkable or that it is bad luck, you are saying that the probability of its happening is low. If you are playing Monopoly and throw three consecutive double sixes, you have a right to be surprised. The chances of that happening are 1 in 46,656. This doesn't mean that it can't happen—only that it doesn't happen very often, and that when it does, it's a surprise.

Now then, would you be surprised to find out that two of the thirty people in your class have the same birthday? Before you answer, you should figure out the probability. Here's how you do it.

Suppose that there were only two people—you and one other person in the class. The chance that you and the other person have the same birthday is approximately 1 in 366. (This ratio is based on the assumption that about the same number of people in the world share each birthday, including February 29.)

Now, add a third person. The chance that the birthday of the third person will match yours or the other person's is 2 in 366. Next, add a fourth person. The fourth person's birthday might match any of the first three birthdays. The chance of this happening is 3 in 366. And so on.

Continuing in this way, you end up with twenty-nine ratios that can be added in the way that fractions are added. Their total gives you the probability.

$$\frac{1}{366} + \frac{2}{366} + \frac{3}{366} + \frac{4}{366} + \cdots \frac{29}{366}$$

The denominators (366) stay the same in this addition problem. The numerators can be added by using a formula that was discussed in Chapter 10:

$$(n + 1) \times \left(\frac{n}{2}\right)$$

Therefore, the probability of two people in a group of thirty having the same birthday is

$$\frac{435}{366}.$$

This very large ratio means that it is almost certain that two people in any group of thirty will share the same birthday. Not only would you not be surprised to find out this was so, you would expect it.

Activity 11.2

A Suppose there is a lottery in your state. A three-digit number is drawn at random. For $1 an adult can buy a ticket picking any number from 000 to 999. If the numbers on the ticket match the numbers drawn, the ticket-holder wins $500. Is that a good payoff? Why or why not? How much of the money the state takes in does it keep?

B Yesterday the lottery number was 444. The chances of that number being drawn were 1 in 1000. What are the chances that the number will be 444 again today?

C Suppose you are taking a test that consists of 100 multiple-choice questions. For each question there are four answers to choose from. Unfortunately, you aren't prepared for the test. In fact, you don't know any of the answers. If you guess randomly, how many questions can you expect to get right?

futurecasting

The future events that people are most curious about are those that cannot be precisely predicted. No one knows exactly what the weather will be on Saturday. No one knows which teams will play in the Super Bowl (until 1–2 weeks before the game) or what the final score will be. No one knows who will win the next presidential election. For events like these, there are no rules you can use to foretell the outcome.

Still, it is possible to make a good guess about such events. Weather forecasters, sportswriters, and political analysts often seem to know ahead of time what is going to happen. But there isn't anything supernatural in their predictions. Experts make guesses based on what they know about their field. Weather forecasters study radar reports and barometric readings. Sportswriters observe practice sessions and look over injury reports. Political analysts interview candidates and study opinion polls. With good evidence and experience, it is possible to look ahead.

In fact, the secret to imaginative forecasts lies not in dreaming up possibilities out of thin air, but in finding out facts and understanding what they mean. For example, when an architect spoke at a conference of home builders in 1990, he told them that in the coming decade, builders would no longer be creating subdivisions—those large areas of nothing but new houses. The architect didn't predict this because he dislikes subdivisions or because he thought it was time for a new idea. He based his prediction on three facts. First, subdivisions use up too much land because each single-family house sits on a large lot. Second, they cause traffic congestion because people have to drive wherever they want to go. Third, they damage the environment because, in most cases, trees and shrubs are cut down to make room for the houses.

This prediction and the reasons for it show how imaginative thinking drawn on facts about the present to come up with ideas about the future. Whether the prediction comes precisely true is probably less important than how it helps people (like the home builders the architect was addressing) plan how to act. Imaginative predictions show people how to look ahead.

Activity 11.3

A   Assume that the age of the subdivision is coming to an end. What predictions can you make about stores and shopping malls? Suppose that you work for a bank and have been assigned to evaluate the application for an enormous loan to build ten huge shopping malls. Will you recommend granting the loan or rejecting it? Why? Write your response in a paragraph and discuss it with your classmates.

B   Pick a field that you know something about. It might be television shows, clothes, auto designs—whatever field you like. Based on what you know about the field, make a prediction about some big change in the coming years. Write your prediction in a single sentence. Then, in a paragraph or two, explain the reasons behind your prediction. Share the paragraph with your classmates, and see what they think of your look ahead.

hindsight

It has been said that historians predict the past. This may sound odd, but predicting the past is actually a common and important activity.

You've probably heard the expression "Monday-morning quarterback." It refers to a person who second-guesses, someone who decides how something should have been done. Of course, the expression applies to activities other than football. Suppose, for example, that you're taking an exam in your English class. You work for quite a while on the essay question and then turn to the multiple-choice questions. But the time ends before you can finish. Then you see that you should have answered the multiple-choice questions first. You're being a Monday-morning quarterback.

What you're really doing is using your hindsight to predict the past. When you decide that you couldn't finish the exam because you started with the wrong question, you aren't just repeating the past; you're explaining it. And the explanation is a prediction. It predicts that the order in which students answer the questions is related to the scores they get on the exam. In other words, your story about how you did on the exam is also a prediction about how other students did.

This sort of predicting is exactly what historians do. A Civil War historian might note that Robert E. Lee won a string of battles until 1862, but that after the Battle of Chancellorsville, Lee was always defeated. The historian might go on to say that the death of the Confederate general "Stonewall" Jackson at Chancellorsville changed the course of the war. This explanation says more than that the war went badly for the South after 1862. It predicts that the battles before Chancellorsville were turned into Southern victories through Jackson's ability as a general.

Of course, predictions cannot stand by themselves. They need to be tested. You could test the prediction about the English exam by asking your classmates in what order they answered the questions and how well they did. The prediction about the effect of the death of Stonewall Jackson could be tested by studying the battles of the Civil War and Jackson's participation in them. Looking for facts to test ideas is one of the marks of a reflective critical thinker. But you can't know what facts to look for until you imaginatively predict the past.

Activity 11.4

Here is a bit of history about which you can make a prediction:

In 1912, people typically traveled across oceans by ocean liner. The ships of the day were large, luxurious, and fast. In fact, people were so interested in how fast the different liners could make the voyage across the Atlantic that one of the front page stories in the *New York Times* on April 13 was an article about the new French liner *France*. It was fast enough to challenge the record held by the *Mauretania*.

Three days before that, the largest ocean liner in the world, *Titanic*, had left Southampton on its maiden voyage. About 2100 people were aboard. On April 14, the *Titanic* received six warnings from other ships about icebergs in the area. The *Titanic* did not alter its course, however, nor did it—thought to be unsinkable because of its sixteen watertight compartments—slow down. At 11:40 P.M. the *Titanic* struck an iceberg. Twenty-five minutes later, the order was given to get the passengers and crew into the lifeboats. There were, however, too few boats for everyone, and there were no procedures for assigning people to boats or for loading the boats. A little over two hours later, the ship went down. Only 705 passengers and crew survived.

Based on these facts, what predictions can you make about the effects of the sinking of the *Titanic* on ship travel? How do you think the tragedy changed the way ocean liners are run? What do you know about shipboard practices and regulations that might be traced to people's responses to this tragedy?

Answer these questions either on your own or with a small group of classmates. Then discuss your answers with the whole class. If you like, you might do some research to find out how accurate your predictions are.

rethinking

A SUMMARY

Imaginative predicting isn't a matter of mystical powers or crystal balls or reading the stars. It's a matter of drawing on what you know to make guesses about what you don't know. One way that you do this is by discovering which laws or rules are involved in events. A second way is by figuring out how likely a particular outcome is. You can also use your experience and knowledge about people and events to predict not only what might happen in the future but also what did happen in the past. Your ability to predict imaginatively can help you better understand events both past and future.

To practice predicting imaginatively, write the end of a story for which you have the beginning. In Activity 9.1B, there are some sentences that outline the beginning of a story. Think about the part of the story that has already been written and predict how the story will end. Write the whole story. You can add to or revise the first part, but don't change the characters or events. Use them as the basis for your prediction of what will happen next.

XII

COMBINING

Some people are imaginative because they think about things that were never thought of before. Gravity, electricity, the "unalienable rights" of humanity—each of these was at one time a new idea in the world.

But a person can be imaginative without creating a new idea. The ability to combine old ideas in new ways is also imaginative. To put a jigsaw puzzle together, it helps if you are able to imagine what the completed picture will look like.

This chapter examines three different aspects of combining. The first is the process of putting together pieces to see what they add up to.

The second is the process of choosing. Sometimes, instead of putting together all the pieces that are available, you evaluate them, using some and discarding others.

Finally, the chapter looks at the unexpected results that combining can yield when facts or materials or ideas are merged. The pieces themselves seem to disappear and something new is created.

putting the pieces together

Reflecting on his childhood, American writer Wallace Stegner recalled the town dump in Whitemud, Saskatchewan. He remembers it, he writes, better than he remembers most things about the town, and he describes some of the "treasures" to be found in it—bedsprings, mattresses, papers, furniture, the skeleton of a horse, some volumes of Shakespeare, dishes, pots and pans, jugs, wagon wheels, a baby buggy, rusty barbed wire, melted glass, lead casing, and even some explosive caps for setting off dynamite.

Stegner writes that he could see the history of the town in the dump. He says,

> I think I learned more from the town dump than I learned from school: more about people, more about how life is lived, not elsewhere but here, not in other times but now. If I were a sociologist anxious to study in detail the life of any community, I would go very early to its refuse piles. For a community may as well be judged by what it throws away—what it has to throw away and what it chooses to—as by any other evidence.

Using his imagination, Stegner could discover the story of each item in the dump and, by combining these stories, he could better understand the people of his town and their way of life.

This way of learning about a society—discovering the remains and then fitting them together to make a whole picture—is how archeologists work. They interpret the bones and ashes in a cave, the funeral furnishings of a pharaoh's tomb, the clay tablets and pots of an ancient village. By combining the clues, archeologists bring back to life societies long dead.

This approach of taking facts and fitting them together is used in many kinds of work. You go to the doctor and say that your nose is running, your head is congested, you feel achy, and you're sneezing. The doctor combines your symptoms and tells you that you have a cold.

A mechanic combines symptoms to diagnose what's wrong with a car; an insurance investigator combines eyewitness accounts and physical evidence to understand how an accident happened; a meteorologist combines pictures from satellites, radar images, and instrument readings to predict the weather. In each case, the available pieces are put together to come up with a whole picture that makes sense.

Activity 12.1

A Use the following letters to make as many words as you can. Use only the letters given, and use them only once in each word. Give yourself a time limit—say, ten minutes. When you finish, compare your list with those of your classmates. Discuss the methods you used to put the letters together. What methods seemed to work best?

r, e, a, s, t, l, c, f, i

B You probably don't have a town dump you can visit, but you can still use Stegner's approach to studying society. What can you learn from a trash can, a dumpster, a landfill, or a recycling center? Find a place where people throw things away. Notice what has been discarded, and use what you discover to imagine what the people are like. Combine your clues to create a picture that makes sense. Write a brief description of what you observed and of what you think it means.

C You are exploring a cave that appears to have been inhabited by an ancient people, thousands of years ago. In the center of one room, you find a circle of ash. Around it you find bear claws (but no bones) and the kind of shells and pebbles that are found in a nearby lake. What do you think this room of the cave was used for? How do you know? Discuss your ideas with your classmates.

choices

A major league pitcher who throws a fastball, a slider, and a curve has to decide when to use each pitch for best effect. He may show all three of them to some batters but only one to others. The question is how to combine the pitches, how to mix them together to come up with a well-pitched game that will keep the hitters off balance.

The ability to choose and combine makes a smart pitcher. It's a lot like the ability of a cook to choose and combine foods or that of a design engineer to choose and combine features of already existing machines in order to invent a new one. In each case, imaginative thinking begins with recognizing what there is to work with—whether it's a fastball, a tomato, or the infrared signal on a television remote control device. By considering the possibilities, the imaginative thinker can discover good reasons for choosing to use some rather than others.

Suppose, for instance, that you are an epidemiologist—a doctor who studies and attempts to control the spread of diseases. Your office receives word from a nearby hospital that four patients have typhoid fever. You know that all four most likely caught the disease from the same source. Your job is to find the source before there are more victims.

You begin by learning all you can about the patients—where they live, how they've spent their time in the last few weeks, what they've eaten, where they buy their food.

But once you gather the information, what do you do with it? How do you put it together?

Well, in this case, you would look for similarities. You would try to find something that each typhoid victim shared in common with the others. Maybe they all live in the same apartment building, or they all ate at the same restaurant. You choose facts that show common connections and, with luck, when you combine those facts, you'll have isolated the source of the disease.

Activity 12.2

A Ancient mythologies contain many examples of imaginary creatures. Often, these creatures combine features of several real animals. The Greek Sphinx, for example, had a woman's head, a lion's body, and a bird's wings. The griffin was supposed to be half eagle and half lion. And the Minotaur was half man and half bull.

Create your own imaginary creature. Invent a creature that you think would be well suited for survival in the world today. Choose its features from real animals (or people). Draw a picture of your creature and label its parts. Or, write a description and explain why this creature is well suited for life in the modern world.

B Choose a television series that you watch regularly and know well. Your aim is to think of an idea for a new episode in the series. Begin by picking out the elements you will combine in your episode. Here are some questions to help you.

1. What characters appear in the series? What makes these characters special or identifiable?

2. What kinds of events does the series deal with? Are these events serious or humorous? Do the episodes end happily with all the problems solved? How are the plots of the episodes alike?

3. What situations frequently occur in the series? Do certain characters get into trouble? Do other characters solve problems? Is there any particular kind of scene—for instance, a chase scene—that usually occurs sometime during each episode?

4. How would you describe the dialogue? Are the characters funny? Do they sound intelligent? What words or phrases do they often use?

5. What settings are used? Are the scenes outdoors or indoors? Are there objects or props that are of special importance to particular characters, such as a car or certain clothes?

Once you have answered these questions, choose the elements you want to combine in your new episode. Think of a new and imaginative way of bringing the elements together. Then, in a page or so, write a summary of the episode as you have imagined it.

the unexpected

A popular parlor pastime of the nineteenth century was viewing pictures through a device called a stereoscope. This device, which resembled a large pair of binoculars, enabled a viewer to look at two pictures of the same scene. What the viewer saw, however, was not two images. Because the pictures were taken from slightly different angles, and because each picture was seen through only one eye, the viewer saw a single three-dimensional image.

You've probably seen a modern stereoscope, probably even looked through one, perhaps at one of the discs that contains a series of pictures that tells a story. You may not have asked yourself, though, exactly what it was you were seeing.

What you see when you look through a stereoscope is not what appears in either of the two pictures. They have height and width, but not depth. Yet the image you see has all three dimensions. The act of combining creates an appearance of depth that doesn't exist in either picture.

You can achieve a similar kind of creativity when you write. You start with words, perhaps only a name. Then you add more words—a description. You add a place and a sequence of events. And somehow, by combining these flat, two-dimensional words, you create a three-dimensional world of people who take on a life of their own.

Activity 12.3

To experience this kind of creativity, invent a character about whom you could write an interesting story or anecdote. Begin by supplying information about the items in the list that follows. Write your information on a separate sheet of paper.

Do *not* think hard about what you will write. Do *not* worry about whether the information makes sense or whether the facts seem to go together. Just put down the first thing that pops into your head. Or, if you like, get some other people to do the work. Ask friends and family members to each fill in a blank or two, and you record the information.

First name	Favorite type of music
Nickname	Favorite movie
Age	Favorite food
Hair color	Favorite color
Eye color	Adjective describing personality
Height	Typical gesture
Weight	Names and descriptions of close
Number of family members	friends
Name and relation of each family	Grade average
member	Favorite school subject
Hobby	Least favorite school subject
Hometown	Job
Favorite season	Religion
Favorite sport	

Combining the information you have gathered, you can now invent a character. You do not need to use all of the information, and you may want to change some of it, but try to use as much as possible. Let the information come together, so that instead of a list of words, you have a three-dimensional, living human being. As you begin to see this person in your mind, think about a problem or conflict he or she would face. Draw this problem or conflict out of the information you have gathered. How the person deals with the problem could be the basis for a short story.

On a separate sheet of paper, describe your character and his or her problem. If you like, you can write the whole story and share it with your classmates. Be sure to share your story with anyone who helped you come up with the information.

rethinking

A   SUMMARY

Combining helps you think imaginatively, giving you a way to recycle facts and ideas. As Wallace Stegner wrote, the town dump was not just a pile of garbage. It was also a museum in which he found the clues to better understand himself and his neighbors. He combined the clues, putting them together to see what they added up to. Combining can also involve evaluating and choosing. And, finally, there are times when the facts, materials, or ideas that you combine merge so fully that they cease to be what they were. You don't see a pair of two-dimensional pictures in a stereoscope, but a single three-dimensional image.

To practice combining imaginatively, put together the clues that follow and write a mystery story. In your story, you must use all of these clues, combining them in a way that makes sense. You may rewrite them, and you can tell the story from any point of view that you like. You will need to add new information, perhaps some new characters, and certainly your own conclusion. When you finish your story, share it with your classmates, and see how they combined the clues to make their own stories.

1. Ms. Richards usually worked on Saturday.

2. Ms. Radetzky complained that Ms. Richards had stolen ideas from her.

3. The security officer in the building discovered the door to Ms. Richard's office standing open at 3:45 P.M. Saturday.

4. The police investigated at 4:15 P.M.

5. Ms. Richards did not learn of the break-in until Monday morning.

6. According to Mr. Long, Ms. Radetzky threatened to "get even" with Ms. Richards.

7. Ms. Richards told the police that her computer and all of her files were missing, including the notes for a new advertising campaign.

8. The guard on duty at the service entrance received a phone call at 12:10 P.M.

9. Ms. Richards told Mr. Long that she was going away for the weekend.

10. The police found no evidence of a break-in, and they concluded that the thief must have had a key.

11. The security officer told the police that Ms. Radetzky worked in her office all morning on Saturday.

12. The president of the company was considering both Ms. Richards and Mr. Long for the same job as vice president.

13. The security officer said that Mr. Long came into the building at noon and left about fifteen minutes later.

14. The service entrance at the rear of the building was open all day Saturday.

15. Both the security officer and the guard carry one master key and keep a spare in their offices.

XIII

CLASSIFYING

When you classify, you put things into groups. It's a common activity. You do it every time you speak. Instead of inventing a unique name for everything you want to talk about, you use words like *rose, whisper, building*. Each of these words stands not for one thing but for a group, or category, of things.

Think of all the buildings you've ever seen. They come in different sizes and shapes; they're made from different materials; they're standing in different places. In fact, it would be impossible to find two buildings that are exactly alike. Yet the same word takes in glass-and-steel skyscrapers one hundred stories high and one-story wooden churches two hundred years old. Both structures can be classified as a "building" because, despite all the differences between them, there are also similarities. Both have been constructed; both have walls, ceilings, and floors; both have doors and windows. The category "building" helps you pick out these similarities. Classifying is a way of making all the differences in the world manageable.

This chapter explores three kinds of classifying. The first is the process of sorting things into groups. The second is the process of dividing something into parts. The last is the process of deciding which things go together and which don't.

grouping

Even as a boy growing up in eighteenth-century Sweden, Carl von Linné loved flowers. So it was natural for him to become a botanist. Like other botanists of the time, he was also an explorer and traveled to little-known regions in search of new plants. To keep track of the plants he discovered, Linné developed a system for classifying them. His system grouped together those plants whose flowers had the same structure. And because his system focused on the number and arrangement of flower parts instead of on, say, size or color, it was both easy to use and consistent. Another botanist who discovered a new plant could tell at once where it would fit in the Linnaean system. In fact, Linné's system for classifying and naming plants made so much sense that it is still used today.

Discovering useful ways to group things is important in scientific work. Of course, grouping isn't something that only scientists do. The ancient Greek philosopher Aristotle classified different forms of government according to whose interests the government served and who ruled. Librarians today use the Dewey decimal system and the Library of Congress system to classify books in an orderly way. And record store managers classify music and put up signs to show customers where different kinds of music can be found.

Regardless of what things you want to group, the way you group them remains the same. You pick out a part or a quality that all of your examples have in common. Stars, for instance, are classified according to their brightness; rocks, according to their hardness; and hurricanes, according to the speed of their winds. You can classify any star, rock, or hurricane by measuring how bright, hard, or fast it is.

By picking out one or more qualities as the basis for your groups, you make sure that the groups are separate without overlapping. Otherwise, you could end up with groups that don't work because each item you're classifying fits into more than one group. Suppose, for instance, that you wanted to classify cars and came up with these groups:

Cars with four doors

Cars that cost more than $30,000

Cars with 6-cylinder engines

Cars that seat five people

Some cars fit into none of the groups, others into all four of them. Obviously, these groups wouldn't work as a system for classifying cars. A system that works will cover all the items and make it easy to see where each fits.

You also want groups that make sense. This means that they help you better understand what you're classifying. For example, when a librarian groups books by topic, she or he is not only arranging them but also saying something important about the books and their purpose. The people who use the books are helped by this grouping. If the books were arranged by color or size, no one would be able to use them because the grouping would not make sense.

Activity 13.1

A You have probably heard of the four food groups—meat, fruits and vegetables, dairy products, and grains. Explain the basis for these groups. That is, how do you know which group a food belongs in? How is this grouping useful? What other ways can you think of to group foods? Discuss your answers with your classmates.

B Working with three or four of your classmates, imagine that you are organizing an auto show. All the major manufacturers will be sending their latest models. How will you group the cars so that you can decide which car goes where? When you have devised a system, share it with the rest of your class. Explain how it works and why it makes sense.

analyzing

You know the parts of speech—nouns, pronouns, verbs, adjectives, adverbs, conjunctions, prepositions, and interjections. These categories are sometimes thought of as ways of grouping words. *Elephant* fits in the noun group, *hurl* in the verb group, *ouch* in the interjection group.

If you think about it, though, the parts of speech are not really categories for grouping words. Instead, they are categories for analyzing speech. The categories have not been created by looking at individual words, but by thinking about how people use words. Suppose, for example, that *furfle* was an English word. What part of speech would it be?

Obviously, you can't tell by looking at it or by hearing it pronounced. If all you have is the word itself, you cannot classify it. To know what part of speech *furfle* is, you have to know how it is used by speakers of the language.

The difference between analyzing and grouping is that when you group, you start with many individual items and make categories by putting the items together. When you analyze, you start with one thing and create categories by dividing the thing into its parts. In both cases, you are classifying: you're showing how one group of things is alike and how it's different from another group of things. For instance, in anatomy, the stomach is classified as part of the digestive system. This classification tells what the stomach's purpose is and links the stomach to the esophagus and the intestines, which are also part of the digestive system. The classification also says that the stomach's function is unlike that of the heart, which is part of the circulatory system, or that of the nerves, which are part of the nervous system. Analyzing the body into systems helps students of anatomy better understand how the whole functions.

People have not only divided the human body into systems but have also divided human life itself. Psychoanalyst Erik Erikson wrote that human development has eight stages, with a specific task or focus at each stage: infancy, early childhood, play age, school age, adolescence, young adult, adulthood, mature age. His categories are similar to, but also different from, the "seven ages" described in the following lines from Shakespeare's *As You Like It*:

> . . . At first, the infant
> Mewling and puking in the nurse's arms.
> Then the whining school-boy, with his satchel
> And shining morning face, creeping like snail
> Unwillingly to school. And then the lover,
> Sighing like furnace with a woeful ballad
> Made to his mistress' eyebrow. Then a soldier
> Full of strange oaths, and bearded like the pard;
> Jealous in honor, sudden and quick in quarrel,
> Seeking the bubble reputation
> Even in the cannon's mouth. And then the justice,
> In fair round belly with good capon lined,
> With eyes severe and beard of formal cut,
> Full of wise saws and modern instances;
> And so he plays his part. The sixth age shifts
> Into the lean and slipper'd pantaloon,
> With spectacles on nose and pouch on side;
> His youthful hose, well saved, a world too wide
> For his shrunk shank; and his big manly voice,

mewling: whimpering. **pard:** leopard. **capon:** chicken. **saws:** sayings and proverbs. **pantaloon:** a skinny, old stock character in Italian comedies.

Turning again toward childish treble, pipes
And whistles in his sound. Last scene of all,
That ends this strange eventful history,
Is second childishness, and mere oblivion,
Sans teeth, sans eyes, sans taste, sans everything.

sans: without.

By classifying the events of life in a sequence of stages, both Erikson and Shakespeare help others to see what life is about.

Activity 13.2

You probably have your own ideas about life. In a few paragraphs, describe the stages or ages of life as you see them. Briefly explain what makes each stage different from the others. When you finish, share your analysis with your classmates.

which ones go together?

One of the familiar segments on the children's television program "Sesame Street" is a game about classifying. The television audience is shown four items and asked to decide which three go together. In one case, the character Big Bird showed four eggs, three of which were small and one of which was quite large. With the help of some children, Big Bird decided that the large egg didn't belong. The other three went together because they were about the same size.

As long as size is all Big Bird is interested in, his conclusion about which eggs go together makes sense. But suppose that size doesn't matter. Suppose that what you are looking for are solid-colored eggs. It happened that two of Big Bird's eggs—the large one and one of the small ones—were white, one was brownish, and one was speckled. If solid color is the basis for your classifying, then the speckled egg doesn't belong. The other three go together—even though they are different sizes.

In other words, there is usually more than one answer to the question: Which ones go together? How you answer the question depends on your reasons for classifying. Are you interested in how big the things are? In what color they are? Are you interested in how they are used? Or where they come from? Or what they are made of? Each basis for classifying may suggest a different answer to the question.

If you are aware of your reasons for classifying, you can be more imaginative in your answer to the question: Which ones go together? You'll see that there is not a single right answer to the question, because the answer doesn't come from the objects you are dealing with. It comes from the way that you think about them.

Activity 13.3

For each of the lists that follow, answer the question: Which ones go together? But don't answer the question only once. See how many different answers you can come up with. Compare your answers with those of your classmates, and explain the reason for each answer.

1. a newspaper, a bulletin board, a novel, a magazine

2. a rowboat, a canoe, a bicycle, a cruise ship

3. Elizabeth I, William Shakespeare, James I, President Bush

4. a baseball bat, a telephone pole, a wooden goal post, a pole-vaulter's pole

5.

6. a banana, a slice of Swiss cheese, a lemon, a lime

7. a thesaurus, an atlas, an encyclopedia, a travel guide

8. a measuring cup, a candy thermometer, a ruler, a wooden spoon

9. a dog, a hamster, a fish, a tiger

10. Beethoven's Fifth Symphony, Bizet's opera *Carmen*, the Beatles' song "Hard Day's Night," Stephen Foster's song "My Old Kentucky Home"

rethinking
A   S U M M A R Y

Classifying is a way of understanding the unfamiliar. When you see a four-legged, furry creature walking down the sidewalk and think to yourself "dog," you're connecting this particular creature you've never seen before to others you've petted, walked, and played fetch with. Because you can classify, you can see more in the world than you would without categories. Old experiences enrich new ones.

Sometimes, classifying is grouping. You begin with a large number of things and sort them into a small number of groups. Other times, classifying is analyzing. You begin with one thing and mentally divide it into parts. And classifying can also be the process of deciding which things go together and which don't.

To practice classifying imaginatively, write an essay in which you report on your trip to another planet. Suppose that you have traveled to a planet that no one on Earth knows anything about. Your particular job on the mission was to study the forms of life in this strange world. In your report, categorize and describe the living things you discovered. Sketching some of these life forms may help you write the report. You could even include the sketches with your essay.

As you prepare for this essay, remember that you do not need to classify life on your imaginary planet as you would classify life on Earth. For instance, you may not want to use the categories *plant* and *animal*. The groups you come up with should fit the creatures you describe. This means that you may need to come up with new names both for the large categories and for the examples that fit in the categories.

XIV

BREAKING HABITS

Habits can be quite useful. If you have a morning routine for getting ready for school, you don't have to plan your actions or think about what you're doing. If you walk to school, you've probably learned a route that you follow without even thinking where you're going. Schedules that you repeat regularly—when you eat your meals, for instance, and what time you go to bed—become habits that help you organize your day.

Without habits like these, you'd have to spend all your time every day deciding what you were going to do next. "Should I put on my right sock first or my left one?" And that would not leave time to do much of anything.

On the other hand, some habits are definitely not helpful. There are times when you need to think about what you're doing, especially when you're trying to think imaginatively. It doesn't help to fall back on a familiar routine. You have to break habits.

Sometimes, imaginative thinking depends on finding a new way to do something—a new method. Other times, the habit that needs to be broken isn't so much a routine as a way of seeing things.

When you're writing, you may find that the habits you need to break are work habits. Instead of assuming that you know what you will say before you begin to write, it helps to think your ideas through as you work. And instead of assuming that the first version you get down is the only way to say something, it helps to look for other versions.

methods

Suppose you have six toothpicks. Can you use them to make four triangles with each side of every triangle a full toothpick in length?

You may have heard this brainteaser before. You may even have tried it. The first triangle is easy:

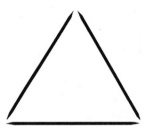

But after that, the puzzle seems impossible. No matter how you slide around the other three toothpicks, you can't make three more triangles. What's wrong?

There is, of course, a trick to this puzzle. That's what makes it a brainteaser. And the trick is that trying to solve the puzzle by sliding the toothpicks around won't work.

Most people working on this brainteaser aren't aware that moving the toothpicks is only one of many possible methods. They get stuck on this one way of trying to solve the puzzle and fail to see that there may be other ways.

The tendency to get stuck on one method is not a problem that you encounter only when you're trying to solve brainteasers. Suppose you're trying to write a story. You have a sliver of an idea for it—perhaps a setting or a line of dialogue or the image of two characters having an argument. But whenever you sit down to start writing, the first line has you stumped. You can't figure out how the story begins. You try one line and then another and nothing seems right.

If you stick to your method—that is, writing the first line first—you may never write the story. But there are other methods. You could begin by writing the middle or the end. You could take your sliver of an idea and start working on it, without worrying about what goes before or comes after. You could just start freewriting and see what comes of it. By breaking the habit of a method that doesn't work, you can begin to think more imaginatively.

Activity 14.1

A Can you solve the toothpick puzzle? If not, here's a hint that may help you. The reason that sliding the toothpicks into different arrangements won't help is that the puzzle can't be solved in two dimensions. You have to create a three-dimensional figure. See if you can figure out how to do it.

B Look at the maze on the next page. The usual method of solving a maze is to begin at the start and trace a path without crossing any lines. What would be an alternative method? Would your alternative be a faster way of finding a solution? Why or why not? Discuss your answers with your classmates. Your teacher may supply a photocopy of the maze so you can actually draw a path.

C Another brainteaser tells of two men who argued about which of them owned the slower horse. They swapped stories, each telling of races his horse lost, but neither was persuaded. Finally, they decided to have a race that would prove which horse was slower.

At the start of the race, they set off slowly, but then, since each rider wanted to lose, he held back his horse more and more until neither was moving at all. They looked at one another and didn't know what to do. They got off their horses and were talking over the problem when a young girl happened by. She overheard them and made a suggestion, which they accepted at once. They jumped back on the horses and raced at top speed for the finish line.

What did the young girl suggest?

(Hint: What is wrong with the method of each man riding his horse in this race? What other method is there of conducting this race?)

definitions

Marjorie Weinman Sharmat has written a number of children's books about the boy detective Nate the Great. In one of them, the break in the case comes when Nate the Great realizes that a box that was used as a seat could also be used to hide something.

Nate the Great's discovery may seem obvious to you, but it wasn't obvious to the characters in the story. And their difficulty in seeing that a place to sit could also be a place to hide something shows another way that thinking can get stuck. It's often hard to free yourself from the usual ideas that you have about everyday objects.

START

END

Consider, for example, Galileo's study of inertia. At the time he lived—around 1600—it was commonly believed that an object moved because a force was applied to it and that when the force was gone, the object would stop. In other words, if you push a wagon, the force of your push will make the wagon roll until the energy is used up, and then the wagon will stop.

Galileo was not convinced that this idea was right. His observation of a swinging lamp and experiments with inclined planes suggested a different idea about why objects move and what makes them stop.

When an object falls, he observed, it picks up speed; it accelerates. He could see this both by swinging a pendulum and by rolling a ball down an inclined plane. When an object is thrown into the air, on the other hand, or when a ball rolls up an inclined plane, it loses speed. This negative acceleration is a mirror image of what happens during falling or rolling downhill.

Now, suppose that you throw a stone not up into the air, but on a horizontal line. The positive acceleration and the negative acceleration are both zero. But because the acceleration is zero, and because the stone is already moving, then it should continue moving without speeding up or slowing down. The stone should keep on going until something stops it. In other words, Galileo realized, the stone doesn't fall to the ground because it runs out of energy. It falls to the ground because the pull of gravity and the friction of the air stop it. What this means, of course, is that if an object, say a rocket, is sent into space (where there is no gravity or air), it can travel indefinitely.

To come to his realization, Galileo had to break a long-accepted habit of thought. He had to forget the usual definition of motion before he could see a new one.

Activity 14.2

A Here is a brainteaser. After you have figured it out, discuss with your classmates the old definition you had to forget before you could see the solution.

A boy is riding his bicycle when he is hit by a car. Within a few minutes, an ambulance arrives, and he is taken to a nearby hospital, where the doctor in the emergency room says the boy must be operated on immediately. The boy is wheeled into the operating room and the nurses begin to prepare him. Meanwhile, the surgeon arrives, takes one look at the boy and says, "I can't operate on this boy: he's my son!"

The surgeon is not, however, the boy's father.

Who is the surgeon?

B In 1795, a Frenchman named Louis Sebastien Mercier published a book called *Memoirs of the Year 2500*. The narrator of the book explains that he slept for 732 years and describes what sort of world he woke up to. Mercier used this plot idea to predict what life would be like in the distant future and to show his idea of a perfect world.

One of the chapters of the book discusses marriage. A "man of letters" explains to the narrator that in the year 2500 women no longer bring a dowry to their husband. The narrator is shocked because in his world— eighteenth-century France—it was expected that a husband would receive money or goods from the family of his bride. Men often chose their wife on the basis of how large her fortune was.

The man of letters says that eliminating dowries has made a better world, because now even a woman from the poorest family can marry a man from the highest class. The man of letters sees other benefits as well:

> We never see a girl proud of her fortune, who seems to do her husband a favor by accepting him. Every man is bound to provide for his wife; and she, depending entirely on her husband, is the better disposed to fidelity and obedience.

The man of letters goes on to say that women have discovered that obedience to their husbands is the only way that women can "secure their happiness."

With three or four classmates, discuss Mercier's ideas about men, women, and marriage. Together, answer the following questions. When you finish, discuss your answers with the other groups in your class.

1. In what ways have the changes in the selection of marriage partners described by Mercier come to pass? In what ways have they not come to pass?

2. How is Mercier's ability to think imaginatively about the selection of marriage partners limited by his definition of the role of women in society?

3. Do you think Mercier would be puzzled by the brainteaser in *A*? Why or why not?

C An old philosophical puzzle asks if a tree falling in the forest makes a sound when there is no one there to hear it. This question is not so puzzling, however, if you think about how you define *sound*. According to one definition, sound is a form of energy. According to another, it is a sensation you are aware of through your sense of hearing.

What answer to the puzzle is implied by the first definition of *sound*? What answer is implied by the second definition?

goals

When you're writing, one of the easiest ways to get stuck is to decide what you want to say. Once you're sure what you think, your thinking stops. George Bernard Shaw wrote:

> When I am writing a play I never invent a plot: I let the play write itself and shape itself, which it always does even when up to the last moment I do not foresee the way out. Sometimes I do not see what the play was driving at until quite a long time after I have finished it; and even then I may be wrong about it.

Shaw was not saying that he wrote blindly or carelessly, only that he didn't make up his mind ahead of time exactly what he would write. He let the ideas unfold as he went along.

Suppose that you were assigned to write an essay for your English class. Your teacher asked you to write about friendship, and you began by deciding that you would say that friends enrich a person's life. Then you thought of three examples of friends who have enriched your life.

With this approach, you would obviously be able to fulfill the assignment. But how interesting would the essay be? Would you learn anything from writing it? Would writing the essay make you think hard about what friendship has meant in your life?

Chances are, if you begin thinking about an essay assignment by deciding exactly what the essay will say, what you write will not turn out to be very imaginative.

A better approach to a writing assignment is to think through the possibilities as you write. Often, it helps to begin with a question—not a made-up question that you don't care about, but a question that genuinely puzzles you. For example, the assignment about friendship might cause you to wonder why you choose some people rather than others as friends. As you think about why certain people are your friends, you may not find a clear-cut answer to this question. But exploring the question will keep you thinking. And the essay you write will have a much better chance of being imaginative, interesting, and worth the time you spend writing it as well as the time others spend reading it.

The experience of writing in this open-ended way is like freewriting. Shaw compared it to taking dictation, as if he didn't make up the characters but just watched them and put down what they said and did.

Activity 14.3

Here's a way that you can experience Shaw's open-ended way of writing for yourself. Choose two people from history. They can be any two people you like. The following names may give you some ideas.

Confucious	Alfred Hitchcock	Frederick Douglass
Babe Ruth	Thomas Jefferson	Orville Wright
Clara Barton	Joan of Arc	Greta Garbo
Chief Sitting Bull	Homer	Harriet Tubman

Once you have chosen the people, get them firmly in mind. Think about how and where they lived and about what they did and cared about. It may help to read a little about each, or to find pictures of them.

Imagine that the two people meet. Don't worry if they didn't live in the same place or time. You can explain the meeting however you like—time travel, a meeting in heaven, or even not at all.

Now, let the two people talk to one another. Imagine that it is really them talking and that you are only eavesdropping. Get on paper the conversation that you hear.

When you finish, share your conversation with your classmates. You might try keeping secret the names of your characters. See if readers can tell from the conversation who is talking.

versions

What is the right way for an actor to play the role of Hamlet? Judging by the hundreds of ways the part has been played over the years, there is no one right way. Some actors make him wild and crazy; others, moody and introverted. A number of times Hamlet has been played not by an actor but by an actress. Many versions of the character are possible, and to present imaginative productions of the play, actors and directors can't let themselves fall into the habit of thinking one version is "right."

Being open to multiple versions is important in many fields. Historians, for instance, deal with different interpretations of events. Was the root cause of the Civil War the disagreement over slavery or the disagreement over the rights of the states? Both versions can be helpful in thinking about what happened to America in the middle of the nineteenth century.

Scientists, too, need to be open to multiple versions. A group of Italian scientists studied pigeons to learn how the birds are able to find their way home. The Italians blocked the pigeons' sense of smell and discovered that this confused the birds. German scientists working on the same problem, however, found that their pigeons weren't bothered by losing their sense of smell.

These contradictory versions helped scientists see that there is no single answer to the question of how pigeons find their way home. Different pigeons in different places adapt in different ways.

The possibility of multiple versions—and the danger of getting stuck on one—comes up when you write. If you put something down without considering alternative versions, you make your thinking less imaginative.

English poet Stephen Spender described how he wrote a poem to convey a vision of the ocean. He wanted readers to see how the waves of the ocean looked to him like the strings of a harp and of how the land was reflected in the water between those strings. The first version of this poem contains these lines:

> The waves
> Like wires burn with the sun's copper glow.

In the next version, Spender rewrote the lines and brought in the idea of music:

> The waves
> Burning as with the secret song of fires

In the next version, instead of the waves burning, it was the day that was burning, and the color mentioned is not copper, but gold:

> The day burns in the trembling wires
> With a vast music golden in the eyes

Spender then cooled the burning to a glow and emphasized the idea of music:

> The day glows on its trembling wires
> Singing a golden music in the eyes.

In the next version, he brought back the comparison between burning wires and the waves:

> The day glows on its burning wires
> Like waves of music golden to the eyes.

Still not content, he wrote another version. This time, he brought back the idea of the day burning, only he changed *day* to *afternoon*, and he continued to work with the idea of music that could be seen:

Afternoon burns upon its wires
Lines of music dazzling the eyes

In the next to last version, he brought back the idea of golden in the word *gilded* and emphasized that the music is seen by describing it as "silent":

Afternoon gilds its tingling wires
To a visual silent music of the eyes

Finally, in the version of the poem that was published, Spender made the wires "silent" (instead of the music) and brought back the word *burning*, but this time to describe the music:

Afternoon gilds all the silent wires
Into a burning music of the eyes.

Because he did not accept a version as final, Spender was able to rework the whole poem—as he did these lines—until he was satisfied with what it said.

Activity 14.4

Even if you are not a poet, you can find new ideas by making new versions when you write. Try it now by writing a paragraph to describe a scene. The scene might be a room, a building, a landscape—whatever you like. Quickly get one version of the description down on paper.

Begin to work on a new version by looking for a word in the paragraph that you might change to make the description clearer or more interesting or more unusual. Think about how changing that word might lead to other changes, and then write a second version.

Revise the second version as you did the first. Ask yourself how the paragraph could be made sharper, more vivid, more exciting. Would it help to rearrange some of the sentences? Is there a detail you left out that could be introduced? Write a third version.

But don't let the third version be the end of it. Read it, reread it, then read it again aloud. Does it sound good? What would make it sound better? Write a fourth version.

By now, the paragraph should look a lot different from the first one. But this doesn't mean that you're done. Does the paragraph say anything interesting? Even a description can tell a story. Does your paragraph tell a story?

Write at least five versions of your paragraph before you settle on one. Share all the versions with your classmates. Discuss how one version led to another, why you settled on the final version, and what new details you became aware of as you created new versions.

rethinking

A   S U M M A R Y

Good thinkers don't get stuck in the same old ruts. They're imaginative because when one method doesn't work, they try a new one. Instead of seeing objects in only one way, they see possibilities. Instead of seeing people as stereotypes, they see individuals. When good thinkers make plans, they're also willing to break them, to follow a better idea. And they don't accept one version as the only version.

   To practice breaking habits of thought, write an essay about a poem that, on the first reading, you did not like. Follow these steps to prepare your essay:

1. After the first reading, write a paragraph explaining as precisely as you can what you do not like about the poem.

2. Read the poem again with these questions in mind: what is the situation in the poem? Who is speaking? To whom? Write a paragraph that answers these questions.

3. Read the poem again with these questions in mind: What happens in the poem? What is the plot? In what ways is the speaker's attitude or tone different in the beginning from what it is at the end? Write a paragraph that answers these questions.

4. Chances are that there is something about the poem—perhaps a word or a phrase—that you do not understand. You may know the meaning of the word but not know what the poet is referring to or what point the poet is trying to make. With that puzzle in mind, read the poem again. Then write a paragraph that tells what puzzled you. If you think you understand the poem better now, include your new understanding in the paragraph.

5. Use your four paragraphs to help you write your essay. As you work on it, decide what its purpose should be—whether you'll evaluate, explain, or simply respond to the poem. It doesn't matter whether you've changed your original opinion or reinforced it. Whatever you've come to think of the poem, let readers see in the essay how you've arrived at the ideas you express.

PART THREE

Nevelson, Louise.
Sky Cathedral. (1958).
Assemblage: wood construction painted black, 11′3½″ × 10′¼″ × 18″.
Collection, The Museum of Modern Art, New York.
Gift of Mr. and Mrs. Ben Mildwoff.

SOLVING PROBLEMS

An odd thing about solving problems is that the process can't be predicted. You can't, ahead of time, break down the solution into easy-to-follow steps. If you could, you wouldn't be working on a real problem.

Having a real problem means that you don't know what to do or think. Suppose you're walking in the woods, trying to find your way back to the main road, and you come to a place where the path divides. Should you take the path that goes left or the one that goes right? This question is a real problem because you don't know which path will lead you where you want to go and because you can't be sure what you should do next. Problems always involve uncertainty.

This doesn't mean that you can't think reflectively about problems. In fact, in Part Three you'll read about seven approaches you can use to think your way toward solutions. But don't expect these approaches to work like the steps in a recipe. You can't solve a real problem by following directions. In problem solving, as in any kind of thinking, you have to exercise your mind.

XV

DEFINING
PROBLEMS

This is a chapter about recognizing problems. You might think the tricky part is solving problems. But recognizing them isn't as obvious as it may seem. Often, you have to figure out what the problem is before you can solve it.

Suppose, for example, that, like Robinson Crusoe, you were shipwrecked on an island. Would that be a problem? Not necessarily. Maybe you like the island. Then you have no problem. As you'll see in the first part of the chapter, you have a problem only if things aren't the way you want them to be or the way you think they should be. A problem begins when you feel a difficulty.

As you become aware of a difficulty, you need to get the facts. What can you find out about this island you've been shipwrecked on? Is it inhabited by cannibals? Is it within sight of land? Is it Manhattan? In the second part of the chapter, you'll read about how getting the facts helps you define a problem.

Finally, in the third part of the chapter, you'll see that an important part of defining a problem is remembering not to jump to conclusions. If you decide that the problem in being shipwrecked is that you don't have any shelter, you may overlook the fact that you don't have any food and water. Keeping an open mind is a basic part of defining a problem.

what's the difficulty?

What pops into your head when you hear the word *problem?* Perhaps an equation in your algebra homework. Or, maybe you haven't decided what to get your mother for her birthday. Or, you might think of a friend who's been avoiding you lately.

These examples show how problems are different and how they are alike. Problems arise in a variety of situations, but they all boil down to a common element: you feel a difficulty that you want to straighten out. And the first step toward straightening things out is to decide exactly what is the cause of the difficulty.

Sometimes the difficulty is a gap between the way things are and the way you want them to be. When you're solving an equation, for instance, you have to get from the form of the equation that you are given to a different form that shows what x equals. But you may not know, at first, what operations you need to perform. That's the difficulty.

Other times, the cause of the difficulty is that the facts you observe don't fit with what you think is true. For instance, you think of Sheila as a close friend, but you heard yesterday that she's having a party, and you haven't been invited. The new evidence clashes with an old idea, and you need to find out how the two fit together. That's the difficulty.

In many situations, it's easy to recognize the difficulty. But this isn't always the case. A major league baseball manager was once asked why his team lost a game, and he replied, "We didn't score enough runs." His answer was certainly true, but it doesn't explain much. In fact, he may have meant it as a joke, as if to say, "I don't know why we lost. I don't know what the difficulty is." In other words, there are times when you feel a difficulty without being able to put your finger on exactly what it is.

Often, what feels like one problem is actually several different problems. For example, the baseball manager may have had a few key players who were injured and needed time to heal, and a few other players who were out of shape and needed to work out. To sort out the difficulties in complicated problems requires careful reflection.

Seeing a difficulty also depends on your point of view. From the point of view of the team that won the game, there was no difficulty at all. And, if the players who lost the game went into it expecting to lose, then they won't see any difficulty in the loss either. The way the game turned out will fit perfectly with their idea about how it was supposed to turn out.

The owner of the team probably won't share that view, however. From the owner's point of view, the difficulty lies in turning a losing team into a winner. There is a gap between the way things are and the way the owner wants them to be.

Recognizing a difficulty, then, is more than just being disappointed. It's a matter either of seeing a gap between where you are and where you want to be or of feeling a conflict between the facts you observe and what you expect.

Activity 15.1

Read the situations that follow and decide in each case what you think the difficulty is. (You may find more than one difficulty.) Discuss your definition of the problem with your classmates. Tell from whose point of view you are looking at the situation and what the source of the difficulty is.

1. The local baseball team has made it to the play-offs, and there are a limited number of seats for the home games available to the general public. The management wants to give everyone an equal chance at getting seats. But the last time the team was in the play-offs—when the seats were sold at the stadium, first come, first served—a number of fights broke out among people waiting in line. The management plans to come up with a different method of selling the seats.

2. A woman is in the last year of studying to be a veterinarian. One of the courses she is taking requires that she perform a surgery on a live, anesthetized dog. She refuses to do the surgery because it is unnecessary and because the dogs are destroyed after the operation. The officials at the university point out that the animals used in the surgeries come from animal shelters and would be destroyed anyway.

getting the facts

You've probably heard that the scores on the major college entrance exams (the SAT and the ACT) are much lower now than they were in the mid-1960s. People have seen this as an indication of all sorts of problems. By itself, however, the downward trend of the scores doesn't indicate a problem at all. It's just a statistic, a fact. Before you can see a problem in it, you have to make sense of it. And before you can make sense of it, you need some other facts. You need the answers to questions like these:

1. How are the scores computed, and what do they mean?

2. How much have the scores declined?

3. How much have the tests changed during the period of declining scores?

4. How do the scores of, say, the top 5 percent in the 1960s compare with the scores of the top 5 percent today?

5. How do the backgrounds of students taking the tests now compare with the backgrounds of students taking the tests in the 1960s?

6. What do the tests measure?

7. What are the tests used for?

8. Has the effectiveness of the tests at predicting success in college changed during the period of declining scores?

9. With what other trends can the declining test scores be linked?

10. Are the declines greater on different parts of the test?

11. Are the declines greater among different segments of the population?

With the facts supplied by the answers to these questions, you could see whether the declining test scores are part of a genuine problem, and if so, how to define the problem.

In this example, to get the facts, you would gather statistics, but getting the facts doesn't always mean finding numbers to work with. Sometimes people can know the numbers and still not have the facts they need to define a problem.

On a test given to a nationwide sample of 13-year-olds, one question asked how many buses would be needed to transport 1,128 soldiers if each bus could hold 36 soldiers. The most common answer was 31, and it's easy to see why. If you divide the total number of soldiers—1,128—by the number who can fit into a bus—36—you get 31, with a remainder of 12.

But though the 13-year-olds showed that they knew how to divide, you might wonder how well they were thinking about the problem. After all, what does that remainder of 12 mean? It means that unless there's another bus, 12 of the soldiers are going to have to walk.

Getting the facts is more than just working with the right numbers: you also have to know what the numbers stand for. Only then can you define a problem.

Activity 15.2

For each of the following situations, write a list of questions that would help you define the problem (or decide if there is a problem). Compare your questions with those of your classmates.

1. Your family receives a flyer from a phone company describing a new offer. For $8 per month, you can make one hour's worth of out-of-state calls. The calls must be made on the weekends or at night. You want to decide if you should take advantage of the offer.

2. In an enclosed glass case, you plant grass and bean sprouts. You also place in the case two earthworms, three beetles, and a grasshopper. After three weeks the blades of grass have tripled in number, the bean sprouts have remained the same, the earthworms and beetles have disappeared, and the grasshopper looks the same. You need to report about these changes.

an open question

The way that a problem is defined can either encourage people to think reflectively or prevent them from thinking at all. For example, nineteenth-century German philosopher Hegel argued that there could be no more than seven planets in the solar system. Philosophy had proved, he said, that seven was the right number. He defined the problem of the makeup of the heavens as a philosophical question, as a matter that could be determined by logic.

Of course, Hegel's definition of the problem was not accepted by most astronomers, who continued to define the problem as a scientific question that would be answered only by observation. They sought to keep open the question of the number of planets, rather than to decide, like Hegel, that the matter was solved.

Hegel's idea seems silly today, but in many situations people fall into the same trap of defining a problem in a way that closes it instead of opens it. They build a solution into the definition—often, a mistaken solution. They block their thinking instead of stimulate it.

A professor of medicine visited his daughter's third-grade class to tell them what it's like to be a doctor. To let them try doing what a doctor does, he asked their teacher to be a patient with a stomachache, and the children took turns interviewing the "patient" to see if they could figure out what the problem was.

Writing about the experience, the professor reported that the third graders acted a lot like medical students, especially in their eagerness to ask what the professor called "hypothesis-based" questions. That means that the children started out with an idea about what the patient's problem was, and then asked a question to see if they were right. One child, for instance, asked if the teacher had eaten lunch. Later, the child explained that he asked that question because he thought maybe the teacher had eaten too much.

After the first case, the professor and the teacher decided to try a second one. This time, one girl didn't wait for the "patient" to say anything at all. She immediately asked, "Do you have any allergies?" Without hearing a word about the "patient's" complaint, she'd already begun to define the problem.

During his visit with the class, the professor tried to help the children see that they could interview better if they waited a while before defining the problem. They needed to begin with questions like "What happened?" or "What's wrong?" They needed to let the problem remain open rather than define it too quickly.

Activity 15.3

A You can play a game that rewards those who work on a problem without defining it too quickly. Form a team with some of your classmates. Your team will play against one or more other teams from your class. With your team members, select from history or from literature a person about whom you know quite a bit. The opposing team (or teams) will try to guess this mystery person. Taking turns, each team can ask another team one question that can be answered yes or no. The winning team is the one that first guesses the mystery person (or persons, if there are more than two teams playing).

B For centuries, astronomers have had to struggle against the earth's atmosphere. The qualities of the air that help shield the planet from harmful rays also distort the dim light that comes from distant stars. In their attempt to deal with this problem, astronomers have placed their telescopes where viewing would be the least affected by the atmosphere—in the desert, on mountains, and, as of 1990, in space.

An astronomer named Edward Kibblewhite has recently come up with a different approach. He has designed a telescope with a rubber mirror that will constantly adjust to the atmosphere. With this new telescope, astronomers on Earth can see greater detail on distant objects—despite the atmosphere.

What Kibblewhite has done is to redefine the problem the atmosphere poses for astronomers. Instead of asking *where* a telescope should be placed so that the atmosphere won't hinder viewing, he asked *how* a telescope could be built so that it would see through the atmosphere.

Think about another problem, say, traffic congestion. List several ways to define the problem. Share your definitions with your classmates, and discuss how the different definitions suggest different solutions to the problem.

rethinking

A   SUMMARY

Problems do not exist on their own. A situation only becomes a problem for you when *you* feel a difficulty, when things aren't as you want or expect them to be. Feeling a difficulty doesn't mean, however, that a problem has been defined. Before you can really get a handle on a problem, you have to get the facts. This means also that you have to keep an open mind and not devise solutions before you know what the problem is.

To practice defining a problem, write a letter to the editor of a local newspaper. Choose a topic that you feel poses a problem for your school, neighborhood, community, or even the country as a whole. The problem doesn't have to be a major issue of national policy. It can be something small like a sidewalk that needs to be repaired or the need for a new course at your school.

In your letter, define the problem. Make clear what the difficulty is and give the facts of the situation. You don't need to spell out the solution, but your definition of the problem should suggest the kinds of steps that you think need to be taken.

Share your letter with your classmates. Then, if you like, send it to the editor.

XVI

SETTING GOALS

Defining a problem isn't the same as solving one; you still have to figure out what to do. And most of the time, your course of action won't be obvious. Suppose, for instance, that you planned a party for ten friends. You ordered enough pizza for ten and then, at the last minute, five more people arrived. The problem is clear: you have more people than you have food for. What will you do?

To act when you face a problem, you have to set a goal. Sometimes this involves breaking a large problem down into smaller problems. You'll read about this method in the first part of the chapter.

In other situations, the best way to set a goal is to consider a number of different possibilities. By weighing the alternatives, you can often discover the best way of dealing with a problem. You'll read about this method in the second part of the chapter.

Finally, as you'll see at the end of the chapter, setting a goal still doesn't mean that a problem is solved. It can happen that, as you work toward a goal, you realize that it won't solve the problem or that there's a different goal that you ought to be aiming for. Be flexible. Be ready to change your goals as you work toward a solution.

big into little

The game Battleship is based on a simple idea. You and your opponent each have a grid like the one below. Keeping your grid secret from your opponent, you decide where your three ships (which occupy three horizontal or vertical grid squares) will be positioned. Then the two of you take turns, each firing a "shot" into one square of the grid. If your opponent's shot hits a ship, you say "hit." If a shot misses, you say "miss." The object is to sink an opponent's ships by hitting all the grid squares on which his or her ships are positioned.

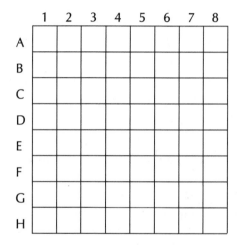

The problem this game poses is, of course, figuring out where the enemy ships are hidden. You could just fire randomly, and if you were lucky, you might win. But that is not an effective strategy. The chances are that you'll lose if you play that way.

A better idea is to break the large problem into smaller problems— literally. Begin by focusing, for example, on the three-by-three square in the upper left corner. With just three shots, you can find out whether there is a ship anywhere in this area. All you must do is make sure that you fire a shot into each horizontal and vertical row, like this:

	1	2	3
A			X
B		X	
C	X		

Continuing in this way, you can methodically check small sections of the grid until you know exactly where your opponent's ships are.

This strategy of breaking a big problem into smaller ones can be used in many situations. A writer of mystery novels, Paul Engleman, described in an interview how he breaks down the problem of writing a mystery. He doesn't try to tackle the whole story at once. Instead, he starts by deciding whether he will write the story in the first person or in the third person. If he chooses first person, he works next on getting a feel for how the narrator talks and what the narrator thinks about. He does this by writing a scene that lets him practice using the narrator's voice. At this point, he doesn't worry about the plot or even whether the scene will be used in the novel. He only wants to get used to the character.

Once Engleman has a character with a recognizable voice and a clear way of thinking, he begins to think about what will happen in the novel. He puts together an outline that roughly describes who does what.

Finally, he takes a situation from the outline—a circumstance that will get the novel moving. He imagines it and begins to write.

By breaking the large problem of writing a novel into smaller ones, Engleman sets reachable goals that help to make the big problem manageable.

Activity 16.1

A Cut out five paper squares, all the same size, say three or four inches on a side. On each square, draw a line from one corner to the middle of the opposite side, as in the picture below. Then cut each square on the line.

Arrange all ten pieces to form a single square.

You can make this problem easier if you break it down. Before you start moving the pieces around, think about how long each side of your square has to be. You know that the area of the big square will be equal to five of the smaller squares. Since the area of any square is equal to the length of a side multiplied by itself, each side of the big square must be longer than two of the small squares, because at that length, the big square would be equal to only four small squares (2 × 2). And the sides of the big square have to be shorter than three small squares, because at that length, the big square would be equal to nine small squares (3 × 3).

Now, how can you arrange the two pieces of a small square to make an edge that is longer than two squares but shorter than three squares?

B Suppose you've been asked to write a limerick, a humorous, five-line poem with the rhyme scheme a-a-b-b-a. How could you break this big problem into smaller problems? What decisions about the limerick should you make before you begin writing?

Discuss your decisions with your classmates. If you like, write the limerick.

alternatives

The script for an episode of "Star Trek: The Next Generation" called for the starship to travel to the edge of the universe. The job for the visual effects co-director, Rob Legato, was to create a convincing picture of what the edge of the universe might look like. Eventually, he used Christmas tree lights reflected off sheets of plastic and filmed them through colored filters and tinted gels.

When Legato was asked if he could have used a computer to design the scene, he said yes, but computer designs take time to develop and are expensive. By comparison, the materials he used were cheap, and the effect took little time to create. Both of these were important concerns for someone working on a weekly television program.

When problems can be solved in more than one way, setting a goal often begins with a look at the alternatives. Legato had to consider different ways of creating a suitable image before he chose a goal. In your everyday life, you also face problems with alternative solutions. Suppose, for instance, that you want to buy two videotapes, but you have enough money for only one. What are your alternatives? You could

1. buy the first one you see

2. buy the one you know the most about

3. decide not to buy either, but rent both of them

4. buy one and borrow the other from a friend

5. decide that you watch enough movies and forget about both of them

6. mention just before your next birthday that you certainly would like these tapes as a present

Without much effort you could add to this list. Then, by thinking about the alternatives, you'd be able to choose a goal that made sense. You might realize that you really wanted one tape more than the other, or that you didn't really need either of them.

This doesn't mean that when you choose an alternative you're just saying, "I like this." This choice should be based on good reasons. Legato chose Christmas tree lights because of their color, their ready availability, and their low cost. They met the most important demands of the problem, which were to create a convincing effect in a short time without spending a lot of money.

Thinking about alternatives can often help you recognize what you need for a solution. Once you see your priorities, you can choose a goal that makes sense because there are good reasons behind it.

Activity 16.2

A Suppose you're planning to go to college but don't know which ones to apply to. Make a list of things you want in a college. You might begin by brainstorming with three or four classmates. From the ideas you produce, choose those that are most important to you. List a few colleges that meet your criteria.

B Suppose you're on a school committee whose purpose is to increase people's awareness of the importance of recycling and of what materials can be recycled. Your job is to come up with a slogan for a recycling campaign. List the points you could make in your slogan and the key words you could use.

Share your list with your classmates and see if they came up with possibilities you overlooked.

Pick out the most important points and key words. Then write your slogan.

changing goals

When the German composer Ludwig van Beethoven wrote his Fifth Symphony, he had a problem with the ending of the first movement. The beginning was dramatic and Beethoven wanted an equally powerful ending.

The first ending he composed didn't seem right. So he made the ending longer, hoping to give it more of a flourish. But this wasn't right, either, and he wrote another finish for the movement, one that was longer yet.

When this ending still didn't seem powerful enough, Beethoven looked back at what he had already written. The problem remained: the music didn't finish with the feeling that he wanted. He realized, though, that the goal he'd set—making the ending longer—wasn't going to solve the problem. What he needed to do was *shorten* the ending. It was weak not because it was too brief, but because it was too long. Once he shortened the ending, the music finished just the way he wanted it to.

For a successful problem solver, recognizing when to change a goal is as important as setting one. But discarding an old goal in favor of a new one can be difficult. The old way of doing something becomes so familiar that it's hard to see an alternative. For several centuries after the Crusades, merchants in western Europe tried to improve trade with the Far East. Travel by caravan across eastern Europe and central Asia was arduous, slow, and dangerous. The goal of most traders was to find a shorter, safer route. But it was the fifteenth-century Portuguese who set a new goal in their attempt to solve the problem of improving trade. By learning more about navigation, they were able to find a water route that replaced the slower overland route.

At the end of the fifteenth century, Columbus tried to change the goal again. He thought that he could improve trade with the East by trying a route no one else had thought of—*west* across the Atlantic. And if the American continents hadn't been in the way, he might have succeeded.

Activity 16.3

A Suppose you're doing library research about the following topics. You want to look at encyclopedia articles for background information, but you can't find an entry for any of the topics as they're phrased here. What other headings could you look under?

1. optical illusions

2. commanders of armies during the Civil War

3. the history of rock music

4. how the common cold is spread

5. the "studio system" of making movies in Hollywood during the 1930s

B You've been asked to write a limerick. You decided to write about a sorceress who makes herself disappear but doesn't know how to make herself reappear. So far, this is what you have written:

> There once was a sorceress named Nell
> Who cast only one magic spell.
> With her wand made of silver,

At this point, you became stuck. What can you do?

rethinking

A S U M M A R Y

When you set a goal, you make a decision about how you will go about solving a problem. Sometimes you set a goal by dividing the problem into steps or by dealing with only part of it at a time. Like a mystery novelist who begins by thinking only about the main character, you focus on something manageable instead of trying to deal with everything at once.

You can also set a goal by evaluating alternatives. As you think about possible courses of action, you can weigh the reasons for choosing one rather than another. If you're thinking about choosing a college, for instance, you can ask yourself which features are most important to you. How much does it matter where the college is? How many students it has? How much it costs? Whether you have friends there? What courses you'd be taking? When you discover your priorities, you can choose a goal that makes sense.

However you set a goal, it's important that you don't confuse reaching the goal with solving the problem. A goal is really a guess about how a problem might be solved, and sometimes the guess is wrong. But as long as you reflect on what you're doing, you can be ready to change your goals when you need to.

To practice setting a goal, write a letter of advice. Imagine that you work for a newspaper as an advice columnist and must write a response for the following letter. In your response, give the letter writer some specific advice about setting a goal that might help solve the problem.

Dear Advice Columnist,
    My problem is my weight. I can't seem to keep it down. I don't have many friends, because I feel shy around people. I'm always afraid they're going to make fun of me. My drama teacher says I should try out for the school play, but I'm afraid to do that until I get my weight down.
    I've tried diets before, but they only work for a little while. What should I do?

                                                    Desperate

XVII

REPRESENTING INFORMATION

Ideas can be expressed in different words. Situations can be seen from different points of view. Being aware of these possibilities pays off when you're solving problems because, if you're flexible, you can often find a clear way to represent information that is otherwise confusing or difficult to grasp. This chapter shows three methods of representing information.

The first method is to put the information into the simplest terms. Often, this means turning words into numbers or equations. A numerical representation can help you solve a problem by getting down to the specific facts you need to focus on.

A second method of representing information is to put it into a chart or a graph. Recording information in this way aids problem solving because a chart can keep track of more information than you can hold in your head at one time. It allows you to see what pieces of information mean when they're put together.

The third kind of representation is models. Some problems are too big or too complicated to be studied as is, but if you make a model—a small-scale example of the problem—you may be able to find a solution that you wouldn't otherwise see.

new terms

On October 16, 1903, the *New York Press* created a stir among its readers with the following puzzle:

> Mary is twenty-four years old. She is twice as old as Ann was when Mary was as old as Ann is now. How old is Ann?

People wrote to the paper with a variety of answers. Some insisted that the puzzle couldn't be solved at all.

What makes the problem difficult is the way it is phrased. The information is not complicated, but the language is confusing. The key to solving the problem is to put the information into terms that can be more easily understood. What exactly does the problem tell you?

First, it says that Mary is twice as old as Ann was at some time in the past. Since Mary is 24, this means that a certain number of years ago (call that number x) Ann was 12. A clearer way to write this idea is to put it into an equation. If you show Ann's age now by the symbol AN, then your equation says this:

$$AN - x = 12$$

It means that if you subtract a certain number of years (you haven't figured out yet what that number is) from Ann's age, the answer is 12.

The second important fact the problem gives is that a certain number of years ago (the same x you've already used) Mary was as old as Ann is now. In other words, if you subtract x from Mary's age of 24, the result is equal to Ann's current age. You can write this as an equation also.

$$24 - x = AN$$

These two equations sum up the information from the problem in a way that makes it easy to figure out the answer. Next, you need to find out what x equals in each equation. By adding x to both sides of the first equation and then subtracting 12 from both sides, you get this:

$$AN - 12 = x$$

By adding x to both sides of the second equation and then subtracting AN from both sides, you get this:

$$24 - AN = x$$

Now all you have to do is put the two equations together. Because the left-hand sides of both equations are equal to x, they are also equal to one another, so you can drop the x.

$$AN - 12 = 24 - AN$$

To see what AN equals, you need to get it alone on one side of the equation. You can get rid of the AN on the right by adding AN to both sides. In the same way, you can get rid of the 12 on the left by adding 12 to both sides.

$$AN + AN - 12 = 24 - AN + AN$$
$$2(AN) - 12 + 12 = 24 + 12$$
$$2(AN) = 36$$

Divide both sides by 2, and you have the answer:

$$AN = 18$$

By putting information into new terms, you can turn a confusing problem into a problem that is easily solved. Takes a little practice, that's all.

Activity 17.1

A A bus travels the thirty miles from Centerville to Newton at thirty miles per hour. How fast will the bus have to go on the return from Newton to Centerville in order to average sixty miles per hour for the entire round trip?

(Hint: In order to answer this question, you should keep in mind what *speed* means. It is distance divided by time. To say that a bus's speed is sixty miles per hour means that the distance it travels divided by the time it is moving is equal to the ratio of 60:1. To figure an average speed of two trips, you have to add the distance of both trips and then divide that number by the time for both trips.)

B You are building frames for a dozen photographs, each of which is ten inches wide and thirteen inches high. All of the frames are two inches wide. In order to know how much lacquer you'll need for the frames, you want to compute the area of each. What is your answer?

(Hint: What is the height of a frame? What is its width? If it helps you, draw a picture. You know that area equals height times width, but remember that the frames are open in the center. You don't need to put lacquer on the photographs—only on the frames. How much space inside the frame does the picture take up?)

keeping track

If you ask your three-year-old cousin how old she is, there's a good chance she'll raise three fingers to answer your question. And if you ask a group of first graders how much six plus two is, there's an equally good chance that some of them will start counting on their fingers. Both groups of children show how helpful it is to have something to look at when you're trying to work out a problem.

Of course, *you* don't need to use your fingers to keep track of facts like these. But you do use other ways of keeping track of more complicated problems. When you want to remember what to buy at the supermarket, you make a list. When you give someone directions for getting to your home, you might write the directions or draw a map. When you play checkers, you don't keep track of the game in your head. You use a board and pieces to keep track of the moves.

Most of the time, it's fairly obvious when and how you need to keep track of something. A person who wants to keep track of a checking account, for instance, needs to write down the amount of each check and each deposit. Sometimes, however, it isn't obvious how to keep track of the facts in a problem.

Suppose someone asked you how often people are likely to have a draw in the game Rock, Paper, Scissors. How would you figure it out? You probably know how to play the game. There is a hand symbol for each of the three objects. A fist stands for "rock." A flat hand stands for "paper." And a hand in which the index and middle fingers are held out, with the others drawn back, stands for "scissors." Each of the two players secretly chooses one of the three symbols and then shows it. "Rock" beats "scissors." "Scissors" beats "paper." And "paper" beats "rock." A draw occurs when both players choose the same symbol. So, how likely is it for two players to have a draw?

To figure out the answer, you have to know what all the possible outcomes are. You might be able to figure this out in your head, because there aren't that many, but if you weren't sure, you could easily represent the facts in a chart. Across the top, write the first player's possible choices. Down the left side, write the second player's. Then, in each box, write whether player 1 wins, player 2 wins, or the players draw. Your chart would look like this:

	Player 1		
Player 2	Rock	Paper	Scissors
Rock	D	1	2
Paper	2	D	1
Scissors	1	2	D

With this chart to keep track of the facts, it's easy to see that there are nine possible outcomes and that three of these are a draw. On the average, the game will end in a draw one-third of the time.

Activity 17.2

Here is a more complicated problem for you to solve. With this one, too, it will help to find a way to keep track of the facts.

In the Robinson family, there are five children—Diane, Phil, David, Ramona, and Elizabeth. Each of them is active in one sport. One plays basketball, one is an archer, one swims, one plays soccer, and one plays volleyball. Use the following clues to figure out the order of the children from oldest to youngest.

1. The archer is the oldest of the girls.

2. The basketball player has all his games on Friday.

3. One of Ramona's older sisters kicked the game-winning goal last Saturday.

4. Diane likes to watch the swimmer, who is the oldest.

5. David is younger than the soccer player, but he isn't the youngest.

6. Diane doesn't use a ball in her sport.

(Hint: Make a chart like the one that follows. Use x's to keep track of what each clue tells you. The first clue, for example, tells you that neither Phil nor David is the archer. So on your chart put an x under each of their names next to *archery*.)

Example

	Diane	Phil	David	Ramona	Elizabeth
Basketball					
Archery		X	X		
Swimming					
Soccer					
Volleyball					

models

In 1766, Sir John Pringle was traveling in Holland with a friend. Part of their journey was by canal boat, and Pringle noticed that the boat seemed to be going slower than usual. When he asked why, the boatman said that the water in the canal was low, because there hadn't been much rain. Pringle then asked if the boat was touching the bottom of the canal, and the boat-man said no, the water wasn't that low.

Both Pringle and his friend were puzzled about why a low water level should slow a canal boat, and the friend, who was Benjamin Franklin, de-cided to investigate the matter. At first, he tried to solve the problem in his head. But he didn't have a sure grasp of the forces involved. So he began asking boatmen in England (where Franklin was working as an ambassador) whether in their experience it seemed that the water level of a canal affected the speed of the boat. They all agreed that it did, but their estimates of the size of the effect were far apart.

Two years after he first thought about the problem, Franklin decided to conduct an experiment. He couldn't very well test real canal boats. They were of different sizes, in canals of different widths. Some of the boats were drawn by horses, others by men. There would be no way to know how much these other differences affected the speed of the boats. So what he decided to do was to build a model canal, one in which he could vary the depth of the water. Then he pulled a model boat through the canal over and over, timing it to see how long the trip took when the water was at different levels.

To make sure that his model boat was pulled with the same amount of force on each trip, he attached a long string to the boat, at the end of which was a coin. The weight of the coin pulled the boat through the canal with an equal force each trip. To time the trips, he repeatedly counted to ten as quickly as he could and used his counting to measure the speed of the boat. He made his measurement more reliable by repeating the experiment many times at each depth and averaging his count for all the trips.

Franklin's experiment showed that shallower water would indeed slow down a canal boat. Two years after he and Sir John Pringle first considered the problem of the effect of water depth on the speed of canal boats, Franklin wrote a letter to Pringle, describing the experiment and its results.

In order to get a handle on his problem, Franklin had to find a way to test it. And the only way he could do that was to build a model. With a model canal, he could control the conditions. He could fix it so that the width of the canal, the size of the boat, and the force pulling the boat wouldn't change. All that changed was the depth of the water. That meant that when the speed of the boat changed, it had to change *because* of the depth of the water. Franklin's model did not explain *why* the depth of water should affect the speed of a boat. (The reason is that there needs to be room for the water displaced by the boat's hull to move from the front to the back of the boat.) But Franklin's experiment did convince him that there really was a connection between water depth and boat speed. And the experiment gave him a way of convincing others, too.

Models aren't always designed to answer a single question. An enormous model in Arizona called Biosphere II has been designed to aid scientists' understanding of how plant and animal systems interact with one another. A glass-and-steel bubble encloses five million cubic feet. Within this space, different terrains have been recreated—desert, ocean, marsh, rain forest, savannah, and farm. By studying what happens in this model, scientists hope to learn more about what is happening on Earth as well as discover how human colonies might be set up on the moon, on other planets, or in space.

Building a model—whether it's a tiny canal or a giant greenhouse—is a way to cut a problem down to a size you can deal with. From a smaller, easier-to-handle version of the problem, you can come up with answers that you wouldn't otherwise be able to see.

Activity 17.3

A Think of a model that would help you answer the following question. Describe the model to your classmates. Or, if you like, create the model, and demonstrate it.

Will an object dropped from an airplane in flight fall straight to the ground, or will it curve on its downward path?

B Form a group with three or four of your classmates. Imagine that your group is working on the Biosphere II project. Come up with a problem or question that the model could help you solve. For example, you could test the effects of increased levels of carbon dioxide on plants and animals. Or, you could find out how people react to being isolated for long periods of time in such an environment. Explain to the rest of your class both the problem and the way in which you would use Biosphere II to help you deal with the problem.

rethinking

A SUMMARY

You can't begin to solve a problem—or even to define it properly—until you get the facts. But, once you gather them, you have to be able to make sense of them, to manage the facts and details so that you can deal with them. A helpful strategy for managing information is to find convenient ways of representing it.

One kind of representation is to find the most concise terms you can put the information into. If, for instance, a problem is about numbers—how many or how much—then turning the sentences into equations will help you see how to solve the problem.

Some kinds of facts can be charted or graphed. Represented that way, the information can be seen all at once and may help you understand the problem better.

A third way of representing the information is to construct a model. Instead of letting yourself be overwhelmed by the real-life problem, you deal with a small-scale, manageable version of the problem.

To practice using representations in your problem solving, write an essay that reports on the personal heroes of the students at your school. To gather information for your report, question twenty or more students about the people they admire. You might ask questions like these:

Whom do you look up to?

Whom do you think of as a personal hero?

What people do you try to be like?

Name two or three people who have made the world a better place.

Name the most influential people you can think of.

If you could switch places with any person, from the present or from the past, whom would you switch with?

After you record the responses to the questions, you'll need to come up with some way of managing the information. How you do this will depend on what you come up with. You may have many names mentioned or only a few. Or, some names may be mentioned more by one group of students than by another. For example, males may have different heroes from females. The facts you have to work with will determine the best way of representing them.

If you find that a chart or a graph helps you make sense of the answers you collect, include the chart or graph in your report. Write more, however, than just a summary of the responses to your questions. Explain what you think these responses tell you about the students at your school.

XVIII

MAKING PROGRESS

Not all problems are difficult in the same way or to the same degree. With some, the difficulty is immediately obvious: you face a dilemma. You might, for instance, have homework from two classes, but time to do only one assignment. In a situation like this, you need to see the problem from a new angle. Only by changing the way you look at the problem can you make progress toward a solution.

With other problems, instead of a dilemma, you face uncertainty. You may have more information than you know what to do with, and you don't know how to get a handle on the problem. A good way to make progress with these problems is to play with the information. Not only does this help you better understand the problem, but you may also hit on a solution that you didn't see at first.

Then there are problems that are difficult not in the beginning but later, as you get into them. At first you seem to make progress and then unexpectedly get stuck. Often, the difficulty arises because the solution involves a complicated series of steps, and some of the steps appear to take you *away* from the goal rather than toward it. You have to be willing to take a step backwards, make a detour, in order to progress toward the solution.

Finally, some problems are difficult because they are cluttered with possibilities. To make progress on these problems, you may find it easier to rule out what won't work than try to immediately hit upon that will.

a different angle

At times, the path to the solution of a problem seems impossible to find. You consider the logical alternatives and realize that none of them will work. What can you do when you face a dilemma?

One possibility is to try what has been called "lateral thinking." Instead of solving the problem in a straight-ahead, logical way, you go at it from a different angle. You redefine the problem. In the book *New Think: The Use of Lateral Thinking in the Generation of New Ideas* by Edward de Bono, the following example is offered:

> Many years ago when a person who owed money could be thrown into jail, a merchant in London had the misfortune to owe a huge sum to a money-lender. The money-lender, who was old and ugly, fancied the merchant's beautiful teenage daughter. He proposed a bargain. He said he would cancel the merchant's debt if he could have the girl instead.
>
> Both the merchant and his daughter were horrified at the proposal. So the cunning money-lender proposed that they let Providence decide the matter. He told them that he would put a black pebble and a white pebble into an empty money-bag and then the girl would have to pick out one of the pebbles. If she chose the black pebble, she would become his wife and her father's debt would be cancelled. If she chose the white pebble, she would stay with her father and the debt would still be cancelled. But if she refused to pick out a pebble, her father would be thrown into jail and she would starve.
>
> Reluctantly the merchant agreed. They were standing on a pebble-strewn path in the merchant's garden as they talked and the money-lender stooped down to pick up the two pebbles. As he picked up the pebbles the girl, sharp-eyed with fright, noticed that he picked up two black pebbles and put them into the money-bag. He then asked the girl to pick out the pebble that was to decide her fate and that of her father.

The situation seems impossible for the girl. If she says she wants no part of the arrangement, her father will go to jail. If she shows the money-lender to be a cheat, her father will still go to jail. And if she saves her father by pulling out one of the black pebbles, she will be forced to marry the money-lender. What can she do?

Activity 18.1

How can the merchant's daughter come at her problem from a different angle and avoid the dilemma? What advice would you give her? Share your ideas with your classmates and see if you can get her out of her difficulty.

(Hint: One way of looking at the problem is to say that the girl's future will be determined by the color of the pebble that she pulls out of the money-bag. Another way to define the problem is to say that her future will be determined by the color of the pebble that remains in the money-bag. How does this redefinition change the girl's problem?)

Activity 18.2

Max Wertheimer, a psychologist who specialized in thinking and problem solving, tells the following true story:

> Two boys were playing badminton in the garden. I could hear as well as see them from my window, although they did not see me. One boy was twelve, the other ten years old. They played several sets. The younger was by far poorer; he was being beaten in all the games.
>
> I heard some of their conversation. The loser—let us call him B—became more and more unhappy. He has no chance. A often served him so cleverly that he could not possibly return the bird. The situation grew worse. Finally B threw down his racket, sat on a tree trunk, and said, "I won't play any more." A tried to persuade him to continue. No answer from B. A sat down beside him. Both looked unhappy.

Wertheimer says that eventually the boys solved their problem and were able to happily play together again. What would you have suggested that they do?

playing

Suppose you've been given the job of mailing a number of gifts. In all, there are seven small boxes. Since they're going to the same address, you're supposed to put them into a larger box. You have two large boxes (of somewhat different size), either of which you can use. How will you decide which box to mail the gifts in?

If you're a commonsensical person, you'll try packing the gifts into one of the boxes and see what happens. You'll probably rearrange them as you go along and begin to see how they fit together. Once you get a feeling for the best way to arrange them, you'll know which box to choose.

It would be possible, of course, to measure each of the gifts, compute the volume of the two large boxes, and determine mathematically the best fit. It would even be possible to write a computer program that would figure out the problem for you if you gave it the dimensions of all the boxes. But going to such elaborate lengths would be silly. It's easier and more sensible to play around with the problem.

Playing with a problem is like freewriting. When you start out, you don't know exactly how you're going to solve the problem. You try out whatever pops into your head, and if it doesn't work, then you try something else.

If you play with a problem long enough, what usually happens is that you gain a better understanding of the problem. Suppose, for instance, that you were trying to create a "magic square." A magic square is a grid in which numbers are arranged so that the sums of all the rows—horizontal, vertical, and diagonal—are equal.

How can you arrange the numbers 1 through 9 in the following grid to create a magic square?

If you started to play with the problem—just putting numbers into the boxes—you'd soon discover two things. First, you'd see that you have to mix up the little numbers and the big numbers. You can't have 1 and 2 in the same row, or 8 and 9 in the same row. Second, you very quickly would realize that you needed to know what sum the rows should add up to. Otherwise, you can't tell if you're on the right track or not.

Both points can help you better understand the structure of the problem. The second one is especially helpful, because it suggests a productive way you can continue to play with the problem. If all the rows are going to equal the same sum, the sum must be some sort of average. One way to get an average is to combine the smallest number, the number in the middle, and the largest number—1, 5, and 9. They add up to 15. With the numbers that remain, can you make two other groups that also add up to 15?

Well, you could use the second smallest number and two numbers between 5 and 9. That would be 2, 6, and 7. They add up to 15 also. And the numbers left over—3, 4, and 8—add up to 15. Now you're getting somewhere. What happens if you put these three groups of numbers into the grid?

1	5	9
2	6	7
3	4	8

You've got your horizontal rows, but you still need the vertical and diagonal rows. Having 1, 2, and 3 in the first vertical row and 7, 8, and 9 in the last isn't going to work. You need to mix those up. Suppose you leave the top horizontal row the same, but rearrange the second and third rows— maybe by putting the 2 under the 9 instead of under the 1. Then you could come up with this:

1	5	9
6	7	2
8	3	4

The solution is definitely beginning to take shape. You've got the horizontal *and* the vertical rows now. All you need to do is to get the diagonal rows right. Playing with the problem made clearer what the problem was and how to solve it.

Activity 18.3

Finish the magic square. (Hint: When you move the numbers around, move whole rows. That way, the horizontal and vertical rows will still add up to 15.)

Activity 18.4

By using the same procedure (and playing around with the numbers) construct a magic square using the numbers 1 through 16.

Activity 18.5

The following drawing shows the main line of a railway running between A and B. The track at C is a spur that is long enough to hold the locomotive and one boxcar. There are boxcars at 1, 2, and 3. The locomotive (at B) is facing east. The problem is for you to move the locomotive to A, at the same time turning it around so that it faces west. When it leaves A, the boxcars should each be in the same position as at the start. (Hint: What representations can you use to help you play with this problem? As you play with it, look for ways that you can recognize whether you are getting closer to a solution. You might, for instance, try solving the problem backwards. Just before the locomotive makes its final move from B to A, where will boxcar 1 have to be situated?)

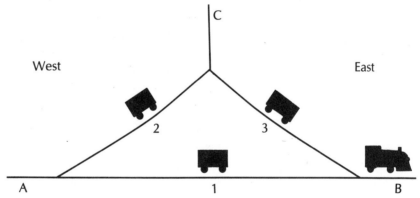

one step backwards

It is said that the shortest distance between two points is a straight line, but there are times when the straight-line path isn't practical. The wagon trains of the Old West didn't cross the plains in a straight line. They followed easy trails and rivers, sometimes making detours around dangerous country.

Problem solving can be like making a cross-country journey, because you don't always head exactly toward your destination. Sometimes, in order to go forward with a problem, you have to take a step backwards. If you're writing a story, for instance, you could begin with the first sentence and keep going until you finished. That would be the straight-line approach. But it would probably make more sense to spend some time planning your story, maybe writing some notes, maybe writing some dialogue and scenes—even if you don't use them later.

It's especially clear when you're revising something that you have to go backwards if you're going to go forward. Revising is all about going back and doing it over until you get it right. When you're crossing out a page that you labored over, it may seem that you've been wasting your time, but chances are that you needed to write that page—just so you could see why it wouldn't work.

Nevertheless, it's hard to take that backward step. When you have a goal in view, it doesn't seem sensible to head the other way. That's what makes some brainteasers tricky. A well-known example is the Missionaries and Cannibals Problem. This problem involves three missionaries and three cannibals who want to cross a river. They have a boat that will hold only two of them at a time. Any of the missionaries or cannibals can handle the boat, but the catch is that if the cannibals outnumber the missionaries on either bank of the river, the missionaries will be eaten.

The problem is to find the fewest number of trips in which everyone can safely cross the river.

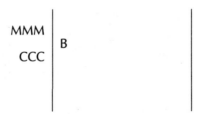

The crossing can be made in eleven trips, but you might have trouble finding the solution because on one of the return trips, you have to send two of the people back with the boat. That may seem like you're taking a step backwards. After all, the idea is to get everyone across the river, not to bring them back. But without this backwards step, the solution isn't possible.

Activity 18.6

See if you can solve the Missionaries and Cannibals problem in eleven steps. It will be easier if you have a way to keep track of your solution. You might record the trips as in the following chart, which shows the beginning situation and one trip. (M stands for missionary, C stands for cannibal, and B stands for boat.)

MMM CCC	B	
MM CC		B M C

Activity 18.7

Here is another brainteaser. Suppose you have three cups. One holds eight ounces, one holds five ounces, and one holds three ounces. The eight-ounce cup is full of water, but you want only four ounces. How can you use these cups (which have no markings on the side) to measure out exactly four ounces?

(Hint: It will help if you record your steps. All you have to do is divide a sheet of paper into three columns—one for each cup. Then, as you imagine pouring the water from one cup to another, keep track of how much water is in each cup. The following chart shows the beginning situation and one step.

8 oz.	5 oz.	3 oz.
8	0	0
0	5	3

The problem can be solved in seven steps. Most of these steps divide an amount of water. In the first step, for example, you divide the eight ounces into five ounces and three ounces. One of the steps in the solution is different, however, and it may seem like a step backwards, because all you do is move the water from one cup into a different cup.)

eliminating possibilities

In Arthur Conan Doyle's novel *The Sign of Four*, the detective Sherlock Holmes and his companion Dr. Watson investigate a robbery and murder. The scene of the crime is a fourth-floor room in which the victim had locked himself with a treasure. The treasure had been found in the attic of the house and had been lowered into the room through a hole made in the ceiling.

When Holmes and Watson arrive on the scene, they break through the locked door, find the dead man's body, and see that the treasure has been stolen. Studying the circumstances, they try to figure out how the criminal could have entered the room. They soon discover that the only window in the room is open, and a rope is hanging from it to the ground. Someone, it seems, climbed up the rope to enter the room through the window and exited by the same route, carrying the treasure. But who, they wonder, let down the rope?

Looking out the window, they see that it would have been impossible for anyone to have climbed up the wall. They decide, therefore, that a second criminal must have entered the room by some other method and lowered the rope for the accomplice. That would answer the question about the rope, but it raises new questions. Watson relates his conversation with Holmes:

> "How came he, then?" I reiterated. "The door is locked; the window is inaccessible. Was it through the chimney?"
>
> "The grate is much too small," he answered. "I had already considered that possibility."
>
> "How, then?" I persisted.
>
> "You will not apply my precept," he said, shaking his head. "How often have I said to you that when you have eliminated the impossible, whatever remains, *however improbable*, must be the truth? We know that he did not come through the door, the window, or the chimney. We also know that he could not have been concealed in the room, as there is no concealment possible. When, then, did he come?"
>
> "He came through the hole in the roof!" I cried.
>
> "Of course he did. He must have done so. . . ."

The best way to solve some problems is to find out what the solution is *not* going to be. If you're playing Twenty Questions, for example, you don't start by trying to guess the secret object right off: "Is it a hubcap?" "Is it a can of paint?" "Is it a peanut butter and jelly sandwich?" These are bad questions because they're too narrow. If the answer is no (as it probably will be), you will have learned almost nothing.

Instead, you begin to solve the problem by asking general questions: "Is it part of an automobile?" "Could you buy it in a hardware store?" "Is it something you could eat?" No matter what answer you get to questions like these, you'll be closer to the solution, because you will have narrowed the possibilities.

This kind of problem solving is one of the ways that doctors diagnose illnesses. To find out, say, that a patient doesn't have a fever means that a great number of diseases can be discarded as possible causes of the patient's complaint. Arthur Conan Doyle, who was a doctor before he was a writer, was trained to use the facts of a case to rule out the impossible. It was a method of problem solving that he passed on to his detective, Sherlock Holmes.

Activity 18.8

Ask a classmate to pick a number from 1 to 100. Try to guess the number. Each time you make a guess, you classmate should tell you whether your guess is high, low, or correct. See how few guesses you need before you get it right.

If you use the right procedure, you can guarantee that you will never need more than seven guesses to get the number. What is that procedure? Discuss your ideas with your classmates.

Activity 18.9

Suppose that you have helped to set up a new VCR. You connected the antenna to the VCR and then connected the VCR to the television. You set the television to channel 3 and put a videotape into the VCR. Finally, you pushed the *play* button. Nothing happened. Using the following information from the instruction manual, decide what's wrong.

When the picture does not appear on the television screen:

- Make sure the television is tuned to channel 3 or 4.
- Make sure the VCR output is connected to the television input.
- Make sure there is a tape in the machine.
- Make sure the power cord is plugged in firmly.
- If you're trying to receive a television broadcast, make sure the antenna is properly connected to the VCR.

rethinking

A SUMMARY

To make progress in your problem solving, you have to be flexible. Sometimes you need to try lateral thinking—coming at the problem from a new angle. That way you can turn a dilemma into a problem you can solve.

Other times, the best way to deal with a problem is to play around with it for a while. Try a few different approaches and see what happens. You may be surprised at the ideas that come when you aren't looking for them.

You also need to keep in mind that the solution to a problem may not appear the way you expect it to. You often have to take what seems to be a backwards step to get closer to the solution.

Finally, there are times when the best progress you can make toward solving a problem is to find out what the solution is not going to be. By eliminating possibilities, you gradually make your way to a solution that will work.

To practice making progress in your problem solving, write a story in which the main character escapes from a seemingly impossible situation. You might choose one of the following situations as the basis for your story.

- A baby-sitter has to deal with two small children who won't cooperate.
- A teenager with a limited amount of money to spend has to decide whether to buy a birthday present for a grandparent or a ticket to a concert.
- A high school student is pressured to join a gang.

Use your story to show a realistic, thoughtful way in which the problem could be solved. The solution should not appear out of the blue. Let readers see how the main character makes progress on the problem until it is solved.

XIX

TALKING ABOUT PROBLEMS

Of all the tools that can be used to solve a problem, the most useful is language. As soon as you begin to talk about a problem, you start making sense of it.

But this doesn't mean that talking about problems is easy. When you're working with a group of people, it takes patience to listen to the views of everyone, but that's what you have to do. Talking through a problem requires a lot of listening.

If the people you're working with don't share your views, you have to listen even more carefully to find agreement on a solution. Only by understanding the views of others and by being able to express them sympathetically, can you hope to come up with a solution everyone will accept.

Talking about a problem can also help when you're working alone. It may seem silly to talk to yourself, but it helps, even if you say the words only in your mind or if you write them. Thinking about a problem hard enough to put it into words helps you concentrate. And if you ask yourself questions about what you're saying, you can make your thinking sharper and clearer.

working in a group

Among Thomas Jefferson's many accomplishments is writing the Declaration of Independence. But while it is true that Jefferson wrote the first draft, what he expressed was not something that he dreamed up on his own. In his autobiography, Jefferson tells how the Declaration of Independence came to be composed. On June 7, 1776, he says, during a session of the Continental Congress,

> The delegates from Virginia moved . . . that the Congress should declare that these united colonies are, and of right ought to be, free and independent states, that they are absolved from all allegiance to the British crown, and that all political connection between them and the state of Great Britain is, and ought to be, totally dissolved.

The proposition was debated on Saturday, June 8, and on Monday, June 10. Jefferson took notes and recorded forty-six specific points that delegates brought up during the debate. At the end of these two days, the Congress still could not agree on the motion for independence. As Jefferson says, six of the colonies "were not yet matured for falling from the parent stem, [but] they were fast advancing to that state," so

> . . . it was thought most prudent to wait a while for them, and to postpone the final decision to July 1st; but, that this might occasion as little delay as possible, a committee was appointed to prepare a Declaration of Independence. The committee were John Adams, Dr. Franklin, Roger Sherman, Robert R. Livingston, and myself. . . . The committee for drawing the Declaration of Independence desired me to do it. It was accordingly done, and being approved by them, I reported it to the House on Friday, the 28th of June.

The following Tuesday, July 2, Congress passed the motion for independence and began to discuss Jefferson's draft. Some parts were cut and others were added. Jefferson notes especially that Congress took out what he had written about King George's wrongly allowing slavery to continue:

> He has waged cruel war against human nature itself, violating its most sacred rights of life and liberty in the persons of a distant people who never offended him, captivating and carrying them into slavery in another hemisphere, or to incur miserable death in their transportation hither.

Finally, on the fourth of July, Congress came up with a version of the Declaration that most of the colonies could accept. It was a group solution to a group problem, and it reflected the convictions and prejudices of all the colonies. It summed up the long debates of Congress and gave voice to the mind of the people. Proud as he was of the Declaration of Independence, Jefferson did not see it as the achievement of an individual. He did not think of it as something that he did by himself, but as something that the people did. He wrote about it not in the first-person *singular*, but in the first-person *plural*;

> Our Revolution . . . presented us an album on which we were free to write what we pleased. We had no occasion to search into musty records, to hunt up royal parchments, or to investigate the laws and institutions of a semi-barbarous ancestry. We appealed to those of nature, and found them engraved on our hearts.

The general problem of whether to declare independence and the specific problem of how to do it could not be solved by one person working alone. The problems had to be talked over, discussed, and debated so that the solutions would reflect the views of the people as a whole.

The problems that must be solved by a group of people working together are usually not so momentous as the founding of a nation, but the key to solving them remains the same—communication. If you're a member of a group facing a problem, you have to talk to the other members and you have to listen to them.

Activity 19.1

Form a group with three or four of your classmates. The problem your group faces is to write and perform a short skit (no more than five minutes long). Together you must decide whether the skit will be serious or humorous and what its subject will be. You'll also need to work together to decide how to write the script, and how to practice it, and how to make changes in it. When you've solved your problems and come up with a skit that satisfies all the group, ask your teacher if you can perform it for the class.

finding agreement

Would it be easy for twenty people to pull a rope a few feet? The rope is not tied to anything, and it is not especially thick or long. One person could easily pick up the rope. So, what do you think? Could twenty people pull it a few feet without much effort?

If you suspect that there's a catch to this question, you're right. The twenty people are having a tug-of-war, ten of them on either end of the rope, and they will have to work very hard to pull it even a few feet.

Sometimes, problem solving is like a tug-of-war. You think that the solution is simple and obvious, but others want a different solution, one that runs counter to yours. When this happens, deciding what to do can become more like arguing than problem solving. People can begin to insist on their own ideas about the problem without taking time to reflect on the ideas of others.

But even if you disagree with someone, you can, if you work at it, solve a problem together. What you have to do, first of all, is see the problem as others see it. Express the problem in words that they can accept. Then, look for ways that your version of the problem and their version agree. Out of this agreement, you may be able to find a solution.

Activity 19.2

Form a group with four of your classmates. Each person in the group should select one of the characters from the descriptions that follow. Your problem is this: A group of homeless people have moved into a park in your neighborhood. Their complaint is that they have no safe, affordable place to live, and they are hoping that by moving into the park they can persuade people to do something about their plight. Some of the families in the neighborhood have complained that their children can no longer play in the park because of the crowds and demonstrations going on there. Some store owners in the area have also complained, saying that business has fallen off because customers are avoiding the park. A petition has been presented to the mayor, asking that the police take down the tents in the park and force the people to leave. The mayor must decide what to do about the situation.

- The *mayor* is up for reelection in six months and wants to listen to and act on the complaints of voters. At the same time, the mayor does not want to use force and cause the situation to become violent. The mayor does not believe the city can afford to build and maintain the low-cost housing that has been demanded.

- A *parent* who lives across the street from the park resents that her three children can no longer go there to play. The parent is also worried about the children's safety when they walk past the park to school. In addition, the parent fears that conditions in the park are not sanitary and may lead to disease.

- The *owner of a hardware store* near the park has had business drop off fifty percent since the demonstration began. The store owner feels that the mayor should pay attention to the welfare of the city's taxpayers.

- The *homeless parent* of three has moved into the park because he has no place to turn. Working for minimum wage, the homeless parent has been unable to pay rent and was evicted from his last apartment.

- The *newspaper editor*, who opposes the mayor's reelection, feels that the mayor has been insensitive to the needs of the poor. The editor has said that the mayor is simply trying to get someone else (such as the state or federal government) to deal with the problem.

Have each member of your group take the role of one of the characters. Discuss the problem until you arrive at a solution or until the mayor decides that no solution can be reached and that the homeless people will be either allowed to stay in the park or evicted.

Share the results of your discussion with your classmates and see what results they came up with.

talking to yourself

One way of working out a problem on your own is to talk yourself through it. Forcing yourself to put the situation into words helps you concentrate. And, because putting the situation into words makes the issues clearer, you can question your ideas more easily. It's like having a conversation with yourself. You work your way to a solution by asking yourself tough questions and then looking hard for the answers.

American philosopher and educator John Dewey collected everyday examples of this process from his students. This is how one of his students talked through a problem:

> In washing tumblers in hot soapsuds and placing them mouth downward on a plate, bubbles appeared on the outside of the mouth of the tumblers and then went inside. Why? The presence of bubbles suggests air, which I note must come from inside the tumbler. I see that the soapy water on the plate prevents escape of the air save as it

may be caught in bubbles. But why should air leave the tumbler? There was no substance entering to force it out. It must have expanded. It expands by increase of heat or by decrease of pressure, or by both. Could the air have become heated after the tumbler was taken from the hot suds? Clearly not the air that was already entangled in the water. If heated air was the cause, cold air must have entered in transferring the tumblers from the suds to the plate. I test to see if this supposition is true by taking several more tumblers out. Some I shake so as to make sure of trapping cold air in them. Some I take out holding mouth downward in order to prevent cold air from entering. Bubbles appear on the outside of every one of the former and on none of the latter. I must be right in my inference. Air from the outside must have been expanded by the heat of the tumbler, which explains the appearance of bubbles on the outside.

But why do they then go inside? Cold contracts. The tumbler cooled and also the air inside it. Tension was removed, and hence bubbles appeared inside. To be sure of this, I test by placing a cup of ice on the tumbler while the bubbles are still forming outside. They soon reverse.

The hardest part of talking through a problem on your own is being tough enough on yourself. The process will only work if you think about each idea and try to find fault with it. Unless you ask yourself challenging questions, the answers you come up with are likely to fall short of genuinely solving the problem.

Activity 19.3

Suppose you are in a supermarket checkout line. You've just paid for the groceries with a ten-dollar bill, but the clerk is giving you change for a twenty-dollar bill. Do you keep the money or tell the clerk about the mistake?

Use the question-and-answer method to talk your way through this problem. Write down your thoughts. Share what you write with your classmates and see how they think their way through the same problem.

rethinking

A SUMMARY

A good way to solve problems is to talk about them. When you have to put ideas into words, you find out what you really think about a subject.

Talking out a problem is critical, of course, if the problem is not yours alone but one that you share with others. Only through communication can a group work together toward a solution.

And when the members of a group disagree over a problem, communication becomes even more important. If you don't listen to one another and try to understand the different points of view, your attempts at problem solving soon turn into an argument.

Even when you're working alone on a problem, you can still talk it through. Questioning yourself about the problem forces you to think more clearly and to figure out how the problem can be solved.

To practice talking about problems, write an essay that interprets or explains an event that is surprising or unlikely. The event could be a physical one—like the soap bubble explanation in this chapter—or it could be something that someone did. Your essay should explore all the causes for the event that you can think of. For instance, if you were writing about why an outfielder dropped an easy fly ball, you might consider whether the sun was a factor, whether the outfielder had been paying attention, whether the grass was slippery or the ground uneven. In your essay, question yourself about each possibility and write your answers. Lead your reader (and yourself) to a final interpretation or explanation that you find convincing.

XX

UNDERSTANDING
ANALOGIES

Sometimes, you don't really work out the solution to a problem. It just comes to you—perhaps while you're waiting for a bus or vacuuming the carpeting. Such moments of inspiration are often the result of analogic thinking. You compare your problem to a different but similar problem and, suddenly, there's the solution.

Sir Isaac Newton, so a famous story goes, was sitting under a tree, pondering how the universe was held together, when an apple dropped from the tree and hit him on the head. Newton made an analogy between the falling apple and the universal attraction objects have for each other and discovered the theory of gravitation. Whether this event really took place is not as important as the process of thinking it illustrates.

On a more ordinary level, if you guess how the word *sought* is spelled by remembering how the word *brought* is spelled, you are, like Newton, using analogy to solve a problem.

A special kind of analogy is the *metaphor*. Here a word or a phrase, referring to one object, is used to refer to another object in order to suggest similarities. An old song begins, "Life is just a bowl of cherries." The metaphor "bowl of cherries" is meant to suggest the sweetness and freshness of life. Taking a different view, another writer says, "Life is a tale told by an idiot, full of sound and fury, signifying nothing."

Although both analogy and metaphor rely on comparisons, an analogy is pretty straightforward, while a metaphor is more suggestive and compressed, taking in a lot of thought in a single phrase.

Analogy and metaphor can help you solve problems by helping you get inside them. If you were a physician, for example, you might try to understand the nature of a disease by adopting the point of view of the virus that causes it. Getting into a problem is a way to use imaginative thinking to solve it.

sudden insight

A metaphor is a figure of speech that brings ideas together. When Shakespeare's Portia speaks of mercy in the following lines from *The Merchant of Venice*, she uses two metaphors:

> It is enthroned in the hearts of kings,
> It is an attribute to God himself;
> And earthly power doth then show likest God's
> When mercy seasons justice.

To say that mercy is "enthroned" brings to mind a king on a throne, a sovereign ruler. The power of mercy to govern conduct is compared to the power of a king to rule a land.

The word *seasons* is a second metaphor. The addition of seasoning, say, salt or pepper, to your food improves the flavor of the food. So, too, Portia is saying, does the addition of mercy improve the quality of justice.

As you can see in these examples, a metaphor says in few words what takes many words to explain. It captures an idea in a single glance.

The power of metaphor can be used to solve problems. When you're thinking about a problem, a metaphor can cause you to see in a sudden moment of inspiration a surprising solution. For example, a scientist who studied genetic diseases was struck by a metaphor one afternoon in an art galley. The scientist, Yury Verlinsky, was at a conference in Israel. He'd been listening to discussions about test-tube babies and decided to go to an art gallery to relax. While there, he spent some time looking at an abstract painting by Spanish painter Joan Miró. The painting showed a red circle and a yellow circle. Beneath the red one floated a small, thin, black circle. To Verlinsky, whose mind was filled with thoughts of fetal development and test-tube babies, the large circles looked like eggs—human eggs. And he began to wonder if the red circle turned into the yellow one after it pushed out the small black circle. Recalling this moment, he said, "I took a business card from my wallet, and scribbled down the idea so I wouldn't forget."

Verlinsky wrote down just two words—"polar body." The polar body is the extra set of chromosomes that a human egg ejects before the egg can become a fetus. What Verlinsky had suddenly seen was that by testing the polar body for genetic disease, he could tell prospective parents whether their baby would be free of genetic disease—before the baby had even been conceived. In Miró's painting he had seen a metaphor for a new method of genetic screening.

What the story about Yury Verlinsky says about problem solving is that you never know when you will discover an important metaphor. He didn't go to the art museum because he wanted to continue his work, but because he wanted to get away from it. Often, getting away from a problem is precisely what you need to do if you're going to find a sudden insight.

Activity 20.1

Find a quiet time to reflect. You might reflect on a painting, an outdoor scene, a piece of music, a story—whatever catches your interest. As you reflect, freewrite your thoughts. Put down everything that comes to mind.

Later, read your freewriting. Look for metaphoric insights that might help you solve a problem. Share your findings with your classmates.

Activity 20.2

Think of a problem that you are struggling with (either by yourself or as a member of a group). Write a brief description of the problem and then think of some two-word metaphors that capture what the problem is about. For example, if your problem was to loosen a screw in a hard-to-get-at location, you might come up with these metaphors:

knuckle scraper

slithering steel

double-jointed fingers

Share your list of metaphors with your classmates and discuss what solutions to the problem the metaphors suggest.

(For practice, you might talk about the three different solutions that the examples suggest for the problem of loosening the screw.)

related problems

Alexander Graham Bell said that he was led to inventing the telephone by thinking about the way the human ear works. "It struck me," he said, "that the bones of the human ear were very massive, indeed, as compared with the delicate thin membrane that operated them, and the thought occurred that if a membrane so delicate could move bones relatively so massive, why should not a thicker and stouter piece of membrane move my piece of steel? And the telephone was conceived."

The idea of drawing on one problem (how does an ear work?) to solve another (how could a telephone be built?) seems so obvious you might think that most people readily look for analogies. In fact, people usually have to be told to look for an analogy before they see it. If you hadn't read about Bell, would you have seen the analogy between an ear and a telephone receiver?

The reason that analogies are often difficult to recognize is that the elements of one problem are usually entirely different from the elements of another. At first glance, skin and bones don't seem much like steel. The following two situations may also seem to be unrelated. Read them and see what connection you see between them.

> A small country fell under the iron rule of a dictator. The dictator ruled the country from a strong fortress. The fortress was situated in the middle of the country, surrounded by farms and villages. Many roads radiated outward from the fortress like the spokes on a wheel. A great general raised a large army at the border, vowing to capture the fortress and free the country of the dictator. The general knew that if his entire army could attack the fortress at once it could be captured. His troops were poised at the head of one of the roads leading to the fortress, ready to attack. However, a spy brought the general a disturbing report. The ruthless dictator had planted mines on each of the roads. The mines were set so that small bodies of men could pass over them safely, since the dictator needed to be able to move troops and workers to and from the fortress. However, any large force would detonate the mines. Not only would this blow up the road and render it

impassable, but the dictator would then destroy many villages in re-
taliation. A full-scale direct attack on the fortress therefore appeared
impossible.

*   *   *   *

Suppose you are a doctor faced with a patient who has a malig-
nant tumor in his stomach. It is impossible to operate on the patient,
but unless the tumor is destroyed, the patient will die. There is a kind
of ray that can be used to destroy the tumor. If the rays reach the tumor
all at once with sufficiently high intensity, the tumor will be destroyed. Unfortunately, at this intensity the healthy tissue that the rays
pass through on the way to the tumor will also be destroyed. At lower
intensities the rays are harmless to healthy tissue, but they will not
affect the tumor either. What type of procedure might be used to destroy the tumor with the rays, and at the same time avoid destroying
the healthy tissues?

—HANK KAHNEY

These situations were used in a study of problem solving. Surprisingly,
few people used one to help solve the other unless the idea of looking for an
analogy was suggested to them. But once that idea was suggested, almost everyone began to see connections. Being on the lookout for analogies can help
you find creative solutions to problems.

Activity 20.3

Here are two solutions to the problem of the dictator's fortress. What solutions to the radiation problem do each of these suggest? Discuss your ideas
with your classmates.

1. The general divided his force into small groups, each of which took up a
   position on one of the roads. On a given signal, the forces charged down
   all the roads, safely passed over the mines, and captured the fortress.
2. While considering the situation, the general received information from
   a second spy that one of the roads had not been mined (because the
   dictator needed to use it as a supply route). Massing his forces on that
   road, the general attacked the fortress and captured it.

getting into the problem

In the 1966 science-fiction movie *Fantastic Voyage*, a submarine and its crew that includes surgeons and scientists are shrunk to the size of bacteria and injected into a man's bloodstream. They travel to the brain to perform a delicate operation that cannot be handled by any other surgical technique. From their microscopic viewpoint, the familiar features of the human body become strange and threatening—not only for the crew members but also for the audience. When you read about life at the level of the cell, it seems remote and unreal, but when you see it in action—even the make-believe action of a motion picture—you begin to understand it in a new way.

It's obvious that understanding the points of view of others is part of reflective thinking and problem solving. What's less obvious is that just as you can get inside the minds of other people, you can also imagine yourself where no one has been or ever will be. You can travel through an artery and be chased by white blood cells defending the body.

This kind of imagining provides more than entertainment. When you make the familiar strange, you make it more interesting. Putting yourself (figuratively) into a problem helps you to see the situation in a new way, so it's a good way to learn about things. It's been used, for instance, in the children's books about the "magic school bus," by Joanna Cole and Bruce Degen. In these books, a teacher takes her class on unbelievable field trips into a rain cloud (where the children find themselves each inside a raindrop), inside a human body (where they pass through blood vessels), to the center of the earth, and through the solar system.

The children in the stories are literally caught up in events, so that questions like "How is water purified?" become genuine problems with personal consequences. Swimming through the mixing basin of a water purification system is a lot more engrossing than only reading about one.

The process of imaginatively putting one's self inside a problem has sometimes been called "personal analogy," and it can be used with a variety of problems. Nineteenth-century German chemist Friedrich August Kekulé gained an insight into the ring structure of the benzene molecule by imagining himself as a snake swallowing its tail. Michael Faraday, a nineteenth-century English scientist, formulated his laws of electrolysis after imagining himself within an atom and visualizing its movement. And German-born, American physicist Albert Einstein said that imagining himself riding on a beam of light led him to conceive his theory of relativity.

Activity 20.4

Students in acting classes often imagine and act out what it's like to be, say, a stop sign or a bowl of soup. You can try the same thing yourself. Together with a group of your classmates make a list of inanimate objects. Write the name of each object on a slip of paper. Take turns choosing one of the slips (secretly) and acting out whatever you choose. See how quickly your classmates can guess what you're pretending to be.

Activity 20.5

Suppose that a city has a number of large public beaches that have been littered with bottles, cans, and other debris. The mayor wants to clean up the beaches and has hired your research-and-development firm to design an easy-to-use tool for this job. Imagine that you are the tool. What do you look like? How do you work? Write down your ideas and share them with your classmates.

Activity 20.6

Imagine that you could go on one field trip on the "magic school bus." Pick a subject—something you've studied in school—that you would explore on your field trip. (Remember that the bus can take you anywhere you want to go, and it can change to any size you want.) Write a paragraph describing how the field trip would help you better understand the subject.

rethinking

A SUMMARY

You can improve your ability to solve problems if you draw on your imagination. Sometimes, this means not working too hard on a problem. Instead, let it simmer in the back of your mind. At the same time, though, you need to be on the lookout for metaphors that transform the problem, analogies that suggest ways to solve it, and opportunities to put yourself inside the events. Metaphors and analogies are more than imaginative language you can use to color your writing, they're imaginative thinking that helps you make the familiar seem strange. When you see a situation anew, you don't take the facts for granted anymore. You stop looking past things and begin to pay attention. And that's just when you may gain a sudden insight.

To practice using imaginative thinking to solve problems, write a poem based on a metaphor or an analogy. Begin by thinking of an issue or a situation about which you are uncertain or confused. Perhaps there are two clear-cut sides, and you don't know whether you agree with either of them. Perhaps you have strong but mixed feelings about another person.

Next, think of a metaphor or an analogy that fits the issue or situation you have in mind. A good source of metaphors and analogies is the natural world. For instance, if you were writing about a person who is affectionate but smothering in his attention, you might imagine ivy spreading across a wall until the wall is entirely covered and invisible.

Finally, write a poem that discusses your chosen issue or situation in terms of the metaphor or analogy you discovered. You might begin by describing only the metaphoric image. Then, as you get into the poem, you could begin to show what this image says about your real topic.

Use whatever poetic form suits your theme. You don't have to write rhyming or regularly rhythmic lines if that won't help you say what you want to say. The important thing is that the poem sorts out and makes clear your feelings about the subject.

XXI

RESEARCHING

Problem solving is more than organizing or interpreting facts you already know. Most of the time, you can't solve a problem until you gather some new information.

Suppose you want to find out the homework assignment for tomorrow's history class. You decide to ask Cecile, but you don't know her phone number. Now you need some new information to solve your problem, and the way you get the information is by doing some research. You look up her number in the phone book, or you call a friend who knows her number.

Described in this way, research may sound cut-and-dried, mechanical. But if you're going to do effective research, you have to reflect about what you're doing. It helps, first of all, not to be so narrowly focused that you miss interesting facts. Suppose, for instance, that the friend you call to get Cecile's number happens to know what the homework assignment is. That is an interesting fact that can shorten your problem-solving time.

While you keep an eye open for interesting facts, you also need to be sure that the information you're gathering is correct. If a friend says that maybe she knows Cecile's phone number, you shouldn't count too heavily on the information. Of course, the worst that could happen in this case is that you'd dial a wrong number, but in other situations, acting on incorrect information could lead to serious difficulties.

Another way you can make your research effective is to take some time *before* you begin gathering information to think carefully about the best source for finding out what you want to know. Sometimes the best source is not a reference book—an encyclopedia, a dictionary, an atlas, a telephone directory, an almanac. Other times, the best source is not a book, but a person—an expert who can tell you what you want to know.

Finally, you can make your research effective by keeping it focused. If you call your friend to get Cecile's phone number, and your friend starts telling you where her parents work and where her brother goes to school, you're getting off the track. Although you should be open to interesting information—facts that may help you solve the problem—you shouldn't necessarily take in every fact offered you. If you're sure that a piece of information isn't related to the problem, forget it.

very interesting

When you're solving a problem, you want to gather whatever information will help. Unfortunately, that advice is easier to give than to act on. How do you know what will help?

Often, you don't know. If you decide too soon what information you need, you're likely to overlook something. Instead of looking for a particular answer, solution, or piece of information, you have to be on the lookout for anything that's interesting.

Suppose, for example, that the year is 1928 and you are Alexander Fleming. As part of your work, you are growing bacteria in petri dishes and notice one morning that in the middle of a dish of *Staphylococcus aureus*, a green mold is spreading—*Penicillium notatum*. Around the mold, the bacteria colony is dying. What do you do? Throw the dish away because the culture is ruined?

Well, you may know what Fleming did. As he said later, recalling the incident, "I was sufficiently interested to pursue the subject." In doing so, he discovered a wonder drug.

Alexander Fleming didn't discover pencillin because he was the first person in the history of the world to see mold kill bacteria. In fact, you might say that he didn't *discover* penicillin at all. Fifty years earlier, the English physicist John Tyndall also carried out an experiment during which penicillin mold killed bacteria. Tyndall and Fleming, and a dozen or more other scientists, including Louis Pasteur, observed that molds or fungi seemed to kill some bacteria. Fleming was just the first person to be interested enough to act on the information.

When you're working on a problem, keep your curiosity alive. Look for the unexpected. Look for patterns and explanations. And don't be too quick to assume that a fact is *uninteresting*. After all, a piece of moldy bread might be just what you're looking for.

Activity 21.1

Suppose you're writing a research paper about the influence of the Beatles on the history of popular music. In the *Readers' Guide to Periodical Literature*, you find the following titles. Which ones do you think you should read? What is interesting about the ones you've chosen? Discuss your selections with your classmates.

"Afterthoughts on the Beatles," *Mademoiselle*, August 1964.

"Beatle Man; Manager for Beatles," *New Yorker*, December 1963.

"Beatlemania," *Newsweek*, November 1963.

"Beatlemania Hits the U.S.," *Senior Scholastic*, February 1964.

"Beatles Reaction Puzzles Even Psychologists," *Science*, February 1964.

"Here Come Those Beatles," *Life*, January 1964.

"Hiram and the Animals, Comparison with the Beatles," *New Yorker*, September 1964.

"New Madness; Rhythm and Blues Quartet Called the Beatles," *Time*, November 1963.

"Science Looks at Beatlemania," *Science Digest*, May 1964.

"What Are the Beatles Really Like?" *Seventeen*, August 1964.

"Why the Girls Scream, Weep, Flip," *The New York Times Magazine*, February 1964.

"Yeah-yeah-yeah! Beatlemania Becomes a Part of U.S. History," *Life*, February 1964.

Yoichi R. Okamoto

Activity 21.2

Suppose that you work in the photographic archive of a museum. In the archive are numbers of photos that may be of historical interest, but the pictures are not labeled or identified. One of the pictures is shown above. Your job is to figure out what the picture is about and when and where it was taken. What features of the picture could help you solve this problem?

making sure

One of the obstacles to thorough research is laziness. When a fact is in doubt, it's much easier to take someone else's word for it than to find out for yourself. But until you find out for yourself, you can't be sure.

English writer Rudyard Kipling told the following story about his friend Sir John Bland-Sutton. Sir John, the head of the College of Surgeons, visited Kipling one cold winter day and talked about a lecture he was going to give on the subject of the gizzard, the secondary stomach of birds.

> We were settled before the fire after lunch, when he volunteered that So-and-so had said that if you hold a hen to your ear, you can hear the click in its gizzard of the little pebbles that help its digestion. "Interesting," said I. "He's an authority." "Oh yes, but"—a long pause— "have you any hens about here, Kipling?" I owned that I had, two hundred yards down the lane, but why not accept So-and-so? "I can't," said John simply, "till I've tried it." Remorselessly, he worried me into taking him to the hens, who lived in an open shed in front of the gardener's cottage. . . . We caught an outraged pullet. John soothed her for a while (he said her pulse was a hundred and twenty-six), and held her to his ear. "She clicks all right," he announced. "Listen." I did, and there was click enough for a lecture.

Sometimes, the way to make sure of your facts is to go out, like Sir John Bland-Sutton, and see for yourself. When American artist John James Audubon wanted to paint birds, he didn't read about them or try to find pictures in someone else's book. He went out into the woods and studied birds and sketched what he saw.

Of course, there are times when you can't check a fact for yourself. Suppose you want to know whether Benjamin Franklin really did fly a kite in a thunderstorm or whether Italian astronomer, mathematician, and physicist Galileo Galilei really did drop weights from the top of the Leaning Tower of Pisa. You can't go back in time and check either event for yourself, but you can read about the subject—in more than one source. Find out what experts say about the subject and why they say it. Then, when you make up your own mind, you'll be as sure as you can be.

Activity 21.3

Suppose you want to buy a stereo system. You want a system that will meet your needs, not break down, and last a long time. How can you research your problem so that, when you go to the store, you'll have a good idea about the kind of stereo you want to buy? Make a list of the ways you could check the facts so that you could be sure of making a wise choice. Which method would give you the most certainty? Share your list with your classmates and discuss which methods would be most effective.

Activity 21.4

Using only a sheet of paper, you can research the following question. What do you need to do?

True or false? When an airplane's wing flaps are down, the plane moves downward; when the flaps are up, the plane rises.

getting help

In 1955, a housewife named Esther Pauline Lederer entered a contest to become an advice columnist with the Chicago *Sun-Times*. Her application for the contest didn't make much of an impression. She'd had no experience as a writer, and, although she'd attended college for several years, she didn't have a degree. She hadn't studied psychology, which the newspaper thought was essential training for someone who would be giving out personal advice.

She got a chance, though. She was given fifteen letters and told to write answers. The first one she looked at was about a walnut tree. The woman who owned the tree was upset become some of the walnuts were falling into her neighbor's yard, and the neighbor was keeping them. The woman thought the walnuts were still hers, but the neighbor didn't agree. Who was right?

Esther felt she needed advice from a legal expert to answer this letter. So she called a friend of hers—Justice William O. Douglas, a judge on the United States Supreme Court. She explained the question, and he had a clerk look up the matter. A little while later, Esther had the answer. As long as the neighbor didn't sell the walnuts that fell into her yard, she could do whatever she wanted with them. Esther wrote her answer, including the fact that it came from Justice William O. Douglas.

The next letter was about a marriage between a Catholic and a Protestant. This time Esther got the opinion of a different expert, Father Theodore Hesburgh, the president of the University of Notre Dame.

She answered the other thirteen letters in the same way, consulting with an expert in whatever field the problem was about. A few days after turning in her answers, Esther Pauline Lederer won the job and began writing under the name she is now known by—Ann Landers. Her experience is a good example of the value of research in solving problems. Figuring out who to ask (or where to look) for an answer is sometimes the hardest part of solving a problem.

Activity 21.5

You probably can't call the people Ann Landers can, but you can still get help with your problems. For each of the problems that follow, write down a person or reference you could go to for help. Discuss your sources with your classmates. Which sources will probably be most helpful? Why?

1. About a year ago, you read a magazine article about hang gliding. Now you think that would be a good subject for an essay you're going to write, but you can't remember the title or date of the magazine. What do you do?

2. You're writing about a friend, and you want to use a word that means *stubborn*, but without the negative connotations. What do you do?

3. There's a skunk under your back porch. What do you do?

4. You want to fix up a bicycle that's been sitting in a garage for a couple of years, but you don't have a lot of money to spend on the project. What do you do?

5. You find a map, dated 1806, in your grandmother's attic, and you want to find out if it's valuable. What do you do?

6. You're going for a job interview, and you want to be sure that the way you're dressed will make a good impression. What do you do?

7. You think you want to stay near your home when you go to college, but you don't know much about the colleges in your state. What do you do?

unnecessary facts

To test how good you are at keeping track of information, read through the following brainteaser once. Without looking back at what you read, answer the question at the end.

> You're the pilot of an airplane flying from New York City to Los Angeles. The plane leaves New York City at 6:10 A.M. (EST) with 82 passengers and a flight crew of 7 aboard. After circling the airport for some time, the plane lands in Chicago at 7:58 A.M. (CST). Three passengers get off, and five more board the plane. Following a delay of forty minutes, the plane takes off again. Fifty minutes after take-off, one of the passengers suffers what seems to be a heart attack. Another passenger (who is a doctor) says the situation is a medical emergency. The plane lands in St. Louis, where the stricken passenger is taken to a hospital (accompanied by the doctor). The landing and delay in St. Louis takes an hour, then the plane takes off again, and in two hours and forty-seven minutes the plane is at the gate in the Los Angeles airport.
>
> Now what's the pilot's name?

This brainteaser is tricky because it contains so much information that a person hearing it only once is likely to forget what the first sentence says. After all, that seems to be only a way of introducing the problem. In fact, however, the first sentence is the only one that matters. The rest is irrelevant.

When you're doing research to solve a problem, your aim is not to gather all the information you possibly can. Sometimes, the best research you can do is to figure out what information is unnecessary—and then get rid of it.

Activity 21.6

Turn back to Activity 17.2. It's a problem about the five Robinson children and the sport each is involved in. Using the six clues, you had to figure out what each child's sport was and what order the children were born in. Look over the problem to remind yourself of it.

Then, together with three or four of your classmates, construct a similar problem of your own. Begin with five people (or families or towns or whatever) that have to be matched up with five activities (or house numbers or population rankings or whatever). Write clues that could be used to figure out your problem. The clues should be clear, but don't make the solution too easy. And don't give any more clues than are absolutely necessary. This means that you may need to write and rewrite your clues, trying the problem after each revision to see how it works. When you're done, the problem should contain just enough facts—and no more. Then it will be challenging and fun for anyone you show it to.

Share your problem with the other groups in class.

rethinking

A SUMMARY

To find the solution to a problem, you have to have information. And if you don't have the information at hand, then you have to do some research. It can take many forms—observing, finding materials in a library, talking to experts—but whatever kind of research you do, there are steps you can take to make it effective and helpful.

First, you have to be on the lookout for interesting facts. This means you can't focus too closely on finding a particular fact—you have to be open to discovering things you don't expect.

Second, you have to want to be sure. You can't let yourself settle for whatever seems reasonable. Research a subject thoroughly, until you finally convince yourself.

Third, it's important to keep in mind that for different kinds of problems, different sources are helpful. Taking the time to think about who you can go to or where you can look is an important step in solving a problem.

Finally, you should remember that researching is more than gathering information. A reflective researcher recognizes that some information is unnecessary and that it should be ignored.

To practice using research to solve a problem, write an essay that compares and contrasts the following pair of words:

knowledge / wisdom

To gather information for your essay, consult at least five sources. These might be definitions or quotations in dictionaries or other books, or instances of the words in everyday speech. You might even want to ask someone (whose opinion you value) what he or she thinks the words mean.

In your essay, draw on your sources to explain the meanings of the two words. Give your readers not only definitions but also a feeling for how the words are used and for why the differences between them are important.

PART FOUR

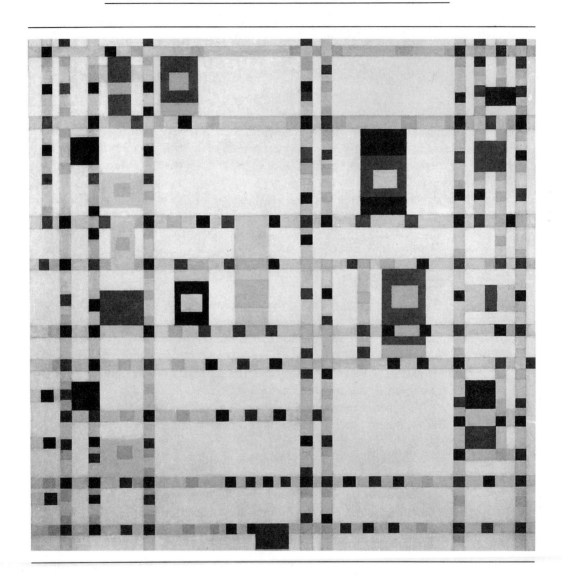

Mondrian, Piet.
Broadway Boogie Woogie. 1942–43.
Oil on canvas, 50 × 50".
Collection, The Museum of Modern Art, New York.
Given anonymously.

THINKING
CRITICALLY

"It is a very great thing," said English poet and critic Matthew Arnold, "to be able to think as you like; but, after all, an important question remains: *what* you think." All thoughts are not equal, and it's easier to think foolishly than to think wisely.

The key to thinking wisely and critically is to be a little like Mr. Spock of the *Star Trek* series, a person who draws no conclusions without sufficient evidence. To be a critical thinker, you have to take the time to examine ideas.

When you think about what someone says or writes, you begin by making sure you understand what the words mean. Then, you decide whether they make sense. You examine the logic behind the words, looking to see what premises or assumptions are being made and testing whether the conclusions really follow from those premises and assumptions. Finally, as a critical thinker, you evaluate what you see and hear: you judge what it means *to you.*

XXII

READING BETWEEN THE LINES

When you think critically about what you hear or read, you decide first what the words mean, then whether they make sense, and finally whether you believe them. The first step in this process—deciding what the words mean—involves thinking not only about what is said in a literal, straightforward way but also about what is only hinted at. To think critically, you have to read between the lines.

One way to read between the lines is to be aware of the values that a speaker or writer is appealing to. And how you judge what is said or written may depend on whether you share those values.

Another way that you read between the lines is to be on the lookout for assumptions—ideas that a speaker or a writer simply takes for granted, like axioms in mathematics. Often, ideas that ought to be examined are assumed to be true.

A third way you read between the lines is to pay attention to your own reactions. A big stumbling block to critical thinking is prejudice, and, in some ways, everyone is prejudiced, because everyone has ideas about what is true and false, right and wrong. If you're going to think critically, you have to be aware of your ideas so that you can give a fair hearing to what others think.

Finally, you read between the lines when you decide on what basis you'll judge what someone says or writes. You don't judge a Presidential address by the same standards that you use to judge a limerick. Setting standards is an essential step for thinking critically.

underlying values

In 1789, the British House of Commons debated a bill to abolish the slave trade. One of the members who opposed the bill, Mr. Norris, defended the business of slave trading. He said the slaves were well treated on the ships. They had water to wash themselves and nice places to sleep, and were even allowed amusement. Before they eat dinner on the ship, he said, "song and dance are promoted." Later in the debate, one of the strongest backers of the bill, William Wilberforce, replied to Norris and others who were against stopping the trade in human lives.

Norris was blind to the evils of slavery, said Wilberforce, and he complained that Norris was not painting an honest picture of the scene.

> The song and dance are promoted, says Mr. Norris. It had been more fair, perhaps, if he had explained that word "promoted." The truth is that for the sake of exercise these miserable wretches loaded with chains, oppressed with disease and wretchedness, are forced to dance by the terror of the lash, and sometimes by the actual use of it. "I," says one of the other [persons who gave] evidences, "was employed to dance the men, while another person danced the women." Such, then, is the meaning of the word "promoted"; and it may be observed too, with respect to food, that an instrument is sometimes carried out, in order to force them to eat, which is the same sort of proof how much they enjoy themselves in that instance also. As to their singing, what shall we say when we are told that their songs are songs of lamentation upon their departure which, while they sing, are always in tears, insomuch that one captain . . . threatened one of the women with a flogging because the mournfulness of her songs was too painful for his feelings.

In making his speech, Wilberforce's aim was, of course, to get others to join him in voting to abolish the slave trade. He based his case on the facts of life aboard a slave ship and on a value that he appealed to but didn't state—the right of all people to be treated fairly. Wilberforce believed that no human being, innocent of a crime, should be punished or condemned to the misery of captivity. This belief in fair treatment is the foundation for his argument, and you have to recognize that if you are to think critically about what he says. You can't decide whether he has provided good evidence unless you know what it is he is trying to prove.

Activity 22.1

In 1990, a Grammy award for Best New Artist was presented to a rock duo who, it later turned out, hadn't done any of the singing on the record album. In performances, the two "singers" had merely mouthed the words while someone else sang. When the truth became public, the award was taken away from the group. A spokesperson for the record company was asked by a reporter if the company found the incident embarrassing. "Embarrassing?" the spokesperson replied. "I don't mean the end justifies the means, but we sold 7 million albums."

What assumption underlies the reporter's belief that the record company would be embarrassed? What value underlies the response of the spokesperson? Discuss your answers with your classmates.

Activity 22.2

There are many values that might underlie a person's desire to lose weight—the pleasure of athletics, good health, popularity, physical beauty, the satisfaction of being fashionable. Think about advertisements you have seen or read for weight loss products—diet plans, low-calorie foods, health clubs, exercise equipment. What value do these ads most often appeal to? (When you are thinking about this question, you should have a few specific ads in mind. Pay attention not only to what is said but also to the settings of the ads and to the models who appear in them.) Share your findings with your classmates.

unstated assumptions

One hot summer afternoon, a deliveryman drove up to a house, got out of his truck, and started up the walk when he noticed a little girl sitting on the steps. "Is your mother home?" he asked her. The girl nodded and said, "Yes." So the deliveryman went back to his truck, slid out a large carton containing a mattress and box spring, and carried the awkward and heavy carton up the steps to the front door. Red-faced and sweating, he pushed the doorbell and waited. No one came to the door. He smiled at the little girl and rang the bell again. Still, no one answered. He waited and rang the bell a third time, and when there was still no sign of anyone in the house, he said to the girl, "I thought you said your mother was home."

"She is," the girl replied, "but I don't live here."

When you read the preceding joke, chances are you made the same assumption the deliveryman made: you assumed the little girl was sitting on the steps of her own home. It's the overturning of this assumption that makes the joke funny.

You can't avoid making assumptions, but when you're thinking critically, it's important to ask yourself what assumptions you and others are making. If you do this, you can decide whether an idea that on the surface sounds reasonable really makes sense after all.

Activity 22.3

Read the following excerpt from a newspaper editorial. What unstated assumptions does the argument depend on?

> The drop-out rate in our city's high schools is at an all-time high. Thousands of seventeen- and eighteen-year-olds are choosing to leave school rather than to complete their education.
> We need reform now. America is falling behind the other industrialized nations. If we want to compete economically in the twenty-first century, we need to turn around this disastrous increase in the number of drop-outs, and we need to turn it around now.

Activity 22.4

What unstated assumption lies behind the following assertion?

> People shouldn't eat refined sugar or bleached flour. Why, do you know that rats and mice won't touch refined sugar and bleached flour? If mice are smart enough to avoid such things, you'd think people would be too.

Activity 22.5

Play the following game with a classmate.

Begin by deciding which of you will play for "odd" and which will play for "even." (The chances of winning are the same for both.) Both of you should place down a coin, covering it with one hand. Then, reveal your coins and see whether you have two heads, two tails, or one of each. If the result is two heads or two tails, the "even" player scores a point; if the result is one of each, the "odd" player scores a point. Play until one of you scores ten points.

At the beginning of each round, as you choose whether you'll show heads or tails, you'll probably try to guess what your opponent will show. What assumptions do you make about your opponent's strategy? How do those assumptions affect your own strategy? After you finish the game, discuss your assumptions about strategy with your opponent.

knowing your own prejudices

The host of the television news-feature program "Sunday Morning" read two letters the producers had received. Both letter writers were indignant over the same segment of an earlier program in which the subject of abortion had been discussed. One writer was angry because of the show's "anti-abortion stance." The other was angry because of the show's "pro-abortion stance."

You may wonder, as did the host of "Sunday Morning," how the two letter writers could have seen the same program and come away with such different reactions. In a sense, of course, what they saw wasn't the same, because it was their own prejudices that the letter writers focused on, not the content of the broadcast.

Some issues are so hotly debated, and people have such strong feelings about them, that even before a word is spoken, minds are already made up. But if you judge what someone says or writes based on your prejudgment of the issue, then you aren't really listening, and you aren't thinking critically.

Of course, it's impossible to ignore your feelings about issues. But you don't have to ignore them—you only have to be aware of them. To be a critical thinker doesn't mean that you have no opinions; it means that you're alert for ideas that may change your opinions.

Activity 22.6

The following excerpt is about "creative sentencing"—the practice of punishing criminals in ways other than sending them to jail. Before you read the excerpt, jot down your views about the sentencing of criminals, the length of prison terms, and prison conditions. Then, after you read the excerpt, list evidence you found that either supports your opinions or causes you to re-think them.

> Many argue that there are good reasons not to ship every criminal off to a jail cell—regardless of his class or color. New York Federal Judge Jack Weinstein contends that sentences for nonviolent crimi-nals should help them get back on their feet, not knock them to the ground. "Very often the person has a job and a family," he says. "What you want to do is work with the healthy part, so that the person isn't utterly destroyed." Professor Monroe Freedman of Hofstra Law School says prison is no more than "graduate crime school. We virtu-ally guarantee they'll come out worse than they went in." William Genego, a professor at the University of Southern California Law Cen-ter, points out that alternative sentences are cheaper for taxpayers. Says he: "There's no reason to spend $10,000 [to jail a criminal] if you can spend $5,000 and accomplish the same objective."
>
> Prison overcrowding is another strong impetus for alternative sentences. With prisons jammed to the rafters in many states, jurists tend to sort out nonviolent criminals when they are considering crea-tive sentences. Some of these punishments are neatly tied to the crime: bumper stickers that identify those convicted of drunken driv-ing and long stays in rat-infested apartments for slumlords. In Califor-nia criminals under house arrest are fitted with electronic sensors that enable authorities to monitor their whereabouts.
>
> Some critics refer to sentences that publicly identify the criminal as a wrongdoer as "scarlet letter" punishments. If rehabilitation, rather than pure retribution, is the goal, these punishments can boom-erang. "The stigmatizing process can go too far," says Albert Alschu-ler, a law professor at the University of Chicago. "We make them out-laws, but we want to integrate them into society at some point."
>
> —ANDREA SACHS

Activity 22.7

The excerpt on the next page—from a *Newsweek* article written by movie producer John Russo—is about horror, or "slasher," movies. Before you read the excerpt, jot down your views about what such movies teach people, about their portrayal of murderers and their victims, and about why people go to these movies. Then, after you read the excerpt, list details from the essay that either support your opinions or cause you to rethink them.

My movies are scary and unsettling, but they are also cautionary tales. They might show witches at work, doing horrible things or carrying out nefarious schemes, but in doing so they convey a warning against superstition and the dementia it can spawn. They might show people under extreme duress, set upon by human or inhuman creatures, but in doing so they teach people how duress can be handled and blind, ignorant fear can be confronted and conquered. My purpose hasn't been to glorify or encourage murder and mayhem, but to give horror fans the vicarious chills and thrills that they crave.

The most powerful and consequently financially successful horror movies—*Night of the Living Dead, The Texas Chainsaw Massacre, Halloween,* and *Friday the 13th*—feature a small cast in a confined situation that is made terrifying by the presence of a monster/madman/murderer. Usually the victims are young, beautiful women. Often the murders are filmed from the point of view of the murderer. For all these reasons, we filmmakers have been accused of hating women and portraying them as objects to be punished for being sexually desirable. Horror fans have been accused of identifying with the psychopathic killers portrayed in these movies and deriving vicarious enjoyment from watching the killers act out the fans' dark fantasies.

But there are two simple, pragmatic reasons why the victims are often filmed from the point of view of the killer. First, it's an effective technique for not revealing who the killer is, thus preserving an aura of suspense. Second, it affords dramatically explicit angles for showing the victim's terror—and the horror of what the killer is doing.

standards of evaluation

Before you decide whether an idea is good, you have to decide what *good* means. The qualities that make something good depend on what you are evaluating. For instance, the qualities that make a brick good are quite different from the qualities that make a pillow good. A good brick is solid, heavy, firm. A good pillow is just the opposite.

The qualities that make something good may also vary with the person doing the evaluating. Let's say you read a magazine article that lists "the ten most livable cities in the United States." That doesn't mean that you should pack up and move to one of them. The author of the article may believe that mild winters make a city livable, but if you enjoy ice-skating, sledding, and cross-country skiing, you won't agree with that.

When you think critically about what people say and write, be sure you have clear in your mind the standards you use to evaluate their ideas.

Activity 22.8

What qualities would you use as standards in evaluating the following? Discuss your ideas with your classmates.

1. a family car
2. a bicycle for use in a Midwestern city
3. a science-fiction movie
4. a pair of shoes for everyday wear
5. a loaf of bread
6. a painting
7. a personal computer
8. a rap song
9. a newspaper
10. a camera to take on a trip to the mountains

Activity 22.9

Each of the following questions offers two ways of saying a single idea. Decide which way is better for the purpose given. Discuss the reasons for your choices with your classmates.

1. Which is more appropriate for a Presidential address?
   a. Without any bad feelings toward anybody, but with good feelings for everybody . . .
   b. With malice toward none; with charity for all . . .

2. Which better expresses a solemn mood?
   a. Four score and seven years ago, our fathers brought forth on this continent a new nation, conceived in liberty and dedicated to the proposition that all men are created equal.
   b. A little over eighty-five years ago, this country was established by some people who liked liberty and equality.

3. Which is more likely to inspire citizens to be firm in the face of a potential invasion?
   a. We shall fight on the beaches, we shall fight on the landing

grounds, we shall fight in the fields and in the streets.

b. We're going to fight the enemy wherever we find them.

4. Which is more clever and thought-provoking?

a. When the gods wish to punish us, they answer our prayers.

b. When the gods wish to punish us they show us how our wishes aren't very sensible.

5. Which is more in keeping with the spirit of democracy?

a. The world must be safe for democracy.

b. The world must be made entirely democratic.

6. Which is funnier?

a. A young lady named Bright could run so fast that one day she left her home, and she got back the evening before she left.

b. There was a young lady named Bright,
Whose speed was far faster than light;
She set out one day
In a relative way
And returned home the previous night.

rethinking
A SUMMARY

When you think critically about what you hear and read, you're concerned with what is implied as well as with what is stated outright. For instance, you take notice of a speaker's or a writer's values and reflect on how those values influence the ideas that are expressed.

You also listen for unstated assumptions—ideas that are taken for granted without being discussed.

In addition, you try to be sensitive to how the ideas of others may reveal your own prejudices. Instead of prejudging ideas—responding positively or negatively without really thinking about what is said or written—you try to set aside your prejudgments, so that you can give ideas a fair hearing.

Finally, you try not to evaluate ideas until you've thought about the standards that you'll use for evaluation. The way you judge a cookie recipe is different from the way you judge a movie script, and you need to be aware of what the differences are and why they exist.

Paying attention to values, assumptions, prejudices, and standards involves reading between the lines. You can practice reading between the lines by writing a critical essay about the following passage from *The Prince* by Niccolò Machiavelli, an Italian statesman who died in 1527. In those days, Italy was divided into five large states and some smaller ones, and these states were often at war. It was a difficult time to be a ruler, or prince, and Machiavelli wrote his book to tell princes how to be successful.

In your essay, write about the values and assumptions you find in the excerpt. Also, be alert for any strong feelings or prejudices the excerpt arouses in you, and discuss these in your essay. Finally, think about the standards you should use to evaluate Machiavelli's ideas. In other words, what do you think he's trying to accomplish?

Here the question arises; whether it is better to be loved than feared or feared than loved. The answer is that it would be desirable to be both, but, since that is difficult, it is much safer to be feared than to be loved, if one must choose. For on men in general this observation may be made: they are ungrateful, fickle, and deceitful, eager to avoid dangers, and avid for gain, and while you are useful to them they are all with you, offering you their blood, their property, their lives, and their sons so long as danger is remote . . . but when it approaches, they turn on you. Any prince, trusting only in their words and having no other preparations made, will fall to his ruin, for friendships that are bought at a price and not by greatness and nobility of soul are paid for indeed, but they are not owned and cannot be called upon in time of need. Men have less hesitation in offending a man who is loved than one who is feared, for love is held by a bond of obligation which, as men are wicked, is broken whenever personal advantage suggests it, but fear is accompanied by the dread of punishment which never relaxes.

—trans. THOMAS G. BERGIN

XXIII

INDUCTION

When you make an inference, you go beyond the facts at hand to reach a conclusion. For instance, from the expression on the face of a friend, you may infer you said something that hurt her feelings. Or, you might hear the slosh of car tires on the street outside and infer that it's raining. Or, you might smell smoke and infer that the bread in the toaster is burning. Anytime you draw a new idea out of the facts at hand, you're making an inference.

These three examples are not only inferences but also examples of inductive reasoning. When you reason inductively, you draw a conclusion that seems likely or probable, but it isn't necessarily so. Take, for example, the inference that your friend was hurt by something you said. The inference makes sense, but suppose you then learned that she was wearing shoes that were too tight. With that new information, your inductive conclusion seems less certain. And that's the way it is with induction: it's always possible that a new fact will cause you to reach a new conclusion.

In this chapter, you'll practice drawing conclusions by inductive reasoning. You'll also think critically about other people's inductive arguments and see that there are two ways to do this kind of critical thinking. The first way is to reflect on the conclusion and on how well it fits the premises, the facts that are offered in its support.

The second way is to imagine what may have been left out of the inductive argument. To do this, you evaluate how reliable and complete the premises are.

drawing conclusions

Inductive reasoning doesn't begin with a conclusion; it begins with premises. A premise is a fact or statement like the following:

- The students in Ms. Henderson's fifth-hour English class have been studying *Romeo and Juliet* for six weeks.
- Those students are all pretty smart.
- Those students all study hard.
- Ms. Henderson is giving a test on *Romeo and Juliet* this Friday.

Now suppose someone asked you whether you think the students in Ms. Henderson's fifth-hour English class will do well on their test Friday. What conclusion would you draw?

Given the premises, you will probably come up with the following conclusion:

Ms. Henderson's fifth-hour class will do well on their *Romeo and Juliet* test.

This conclusion, together with the premises that support it, is an inductive argument.

Drawing conclusions requires effort and common sense. You first have to take the time to dig out the evidence, and then you have to figure out how that evidence fits together. As the fictional detective Sherlock Holmes was forever explaining to Dr. Watson, inductive thinking is mainly a matter of noticing things and looking for the patterns that connect them.

Activity 23.1

English poet John Milton wrote the following sonnet, which describes his reaction to going blind. No one knows exactly when the sonnet was written. Using the sonnet itself and the facts that follow it, construct an inductive argument about the date of the sonnet. The premises of your argument should be facts chosen from those listed and facts you draw from the poem. The conclusion of the argument should state the year in which you think Milton wrote this sonnet.

Present your completed inductive argument to your classmates and see if they find it convincing.

(Hint: What does Milton mean by "Ere half my days"? What does he mean by saying that his "one talent" is "Lodged with me useless"? Does the poem sound like the work of someone who has grown to accept blindness, or does it sound like the reaction of someone still struggling with the loss of sight?)

> When I consider how my light is spent,
>> Ere half my days, in this dark world and wide,
>> And that one talent which is death to hide
>> Lodged with me useless, though my soul more bent
> To serve therewith my Maker, and present
>> My true account, lest he returning chide,
>> "Doth God exact day-labor, light denied?"
>> I fondly ask. But Patience, to prevent
> That murmur, soon replies: "God doth not need
>> Either man's work or his own gifts; who best
>> Bear his mild yoke, they serve him best. His state
> Is kingly: thousands at his bidding speed,
>> And post o'er land and ocean without rest;
>> They also serve who only stand and wait."

1. Milton was born in 1608.

2. His sight, poor since childhood, began getting worse in 1644.

3. During the winter of 1651–52, around his forty-third birthday, his sight failed completely.

4. As early as 1638, Milton had begun planning a great epic, but he didn't finish it until 1665.

5. Milton's father lived to be 84.

6. This sonnet was published in 1673 in a book called *Poems*. In this book, the sonnet is grouped with others that were written between 1642 and 1658, and it is placed between two that were written in 1655. It is known, however, that not all the sonnets are in strict chronological order.

7. Milton died in 1674.

are you convinced?

Conclusions that are reached by induction are common, but the inductive reasoning usually isn't obvious. Writers don't say, "Here are my premises, and here is my conclusion." Instead, you find the reasoning laid out more casually, as in the following excerpt from a *Newsweek* article by Jerry Adler.

Remember how boring and irrelevant history was in school? Remember those dumb dioramas of the first Thanksgiving, the essay question about the Missouri Compromise? Well, someone has figured out a way to make history *even more boring,* and believe it or not, it's a rock-and-roll singer.

Yes, it's Billy Joel, with his fabulous new single, "We Didn't Start the Fire," a nearly five-minute recital of names chosen from the news of the last forty years for no apparent reason other than rhyme. Commit this song to memory, kids, and you are guaranteed to have learned *absolutely nothing. . . .*

The first verse begins with President Harry Truman, who along with Doris Day, "Red" China, and a few of their contemporaries represents the year 1949, Joel having chosen to begin his chronology of the significant events of the universe with the year of his own birth. What, exactly, do we learn from the pairing of Einstein and James Dean? And as for choosing Mickey Mantle for 1957—well, any idiot can tell you he had a much better year in 1956.

Of course, it's up to the teachers to supply this context. If playing a cassette prompts some oaf to sit up and ask, well, who was this Juan Perón character anyway, maybe Joel's efforts won't be a total waste. But if history can be taught this way, why not, say, science?

E equals MC square
  Mammals are the ones with hair
Ozone, pheromone, fiber-optic telephone
  Comet hits us with a blast
Brontosaurus didn't last . . .

And come to think of it, didn't Mick Jagger go to the London School of Economics?

Anyone have a good rhyme for "Adam Smith"?

Parts of Adler's inductive argument are pretty clear. He has three obvious premises:

1. The list of names in the song doesn't convey a meaning.

2. The names are linked without good reason.

3. At least one name is mentioned in the wrong year.

In addition to these premises that are directly stated, another premise is implied. Adler seems to think that learning history is more than memorizing names and dates, that to really learn history, you have to know what people did and why they did it, and you have to have a sense of how events fit together. This idea is a fourth premise:

4. To learn history, you have to know what people did and why they did it.

The four premises lead to Adler's conclusion:

Joel's song won't help anyone learn history.

Does Adler's inductive argument prove that his conclusion is right? Not exactly. Induction can never prove a conclusion for certain. For example, if you throw a softball into the air, you'll feel pretty sure that it will fall back to earth rather than fly off into space. If someone asked why you were so sure, you might point out that you and a lot of other people have been throwing softballs for years, and no one yet has thrown one into space.

But the fact that something hasn't happened in millions of chances doesn't prove that it won't happen next time. It isn't very likely that the law of gravity will cease to operate, but you can't prove that claim through inductive reasoning. The best you can do through induction is make a strong case.

When you think critically about conclusions reached through inductive reasoning, ask yourself whether the argument is convincing. Does the conclusion fit the premises? Are the premises strong enough to support the conclusion?

Activity 23.2

Suppose you are a history teacher. Will you play Billy Joel's song for your class? Why or why not? Discuss your decision with your classmates.

Activity 23.3

An inductive argument is often used as the basis for a course of action. For example, the following inductive arguments could all be used to support the decision to take an umbrella to school. Rate the arguments from the weakest to the strongest. Discuss your ratings with your classmates.

1. March is usually a rainy month, and this is the first day of March. It will probably rain today.

2. I listened to three weather forecasters last night, and they all predicted rain for this afternoon. It will probably rain today.

3. Last week, one of the television weather forecasters said rain was a possibility for today. It will probably rain today, and I'm going to be carrying some books that I don't want to get wet.

4. The weather predictions on station WETT have always been accurate, and last night they said the rain will be heavy most of today. It will probably rain.

Activity 23.4

The statements that follow are taken from an Associated Press report. Suppose that the statements are used as the premises of an inductive argument.

1. Thousands of people in the eastern part of the United States reported seeing a bluish-green light Saturday night.

2. An officer of the North American Aerospace Defense Command said it was not a "manmade object re-entering" the Earth's atmosphere.

3. The national UFO Reporting Center received dozens of calls.

4. A spokesperson from the center said the descriptions sounded like a large, solid meteor.

5. An air-traffic-control supervisor in Washington said the light lasted from twenty-five to thirty seconds, changing in color from white to orange.

6. A TV reporter in West Virginia said the light was still in the sky three hours after the first sighting.

7. The TV reporter said that she had seen many meteors and that this was not a meteor.

Which of these conclusions is most strongly supported by the premises? Discuss your decision with your classmates.

a. A flying saucer visited Earth.

b. A meteor burned up in the atmosphere.

c. Thousands of people saw the same event in the sky.

d. The witnesses probably saw more than one event.

what's missing?

To think critically about inductive reasoning, it isn't enough to look only at what the argument says. You should also consider what isn't said. Sometimes people try to make a case more convincing by leaving out contradictory evidence or by neglecting to mention information that might make the evidence sound less reliable.

For example, the spokesman for an American car company claimed that his company's cars were better than those of a Japanese car company. The evidence for his conclusion came from market research. Two hundred people shopping for a new car in Los Angeles were invited to drive one of the American cars and one of the Japanese cars. Then the people were asked to answer some questions. It turned out that eigthy percent of the people preferred the American car.

At first glance, you may find this evidence pretty convincing. But you need to ask yourself what exactly has been proved. To arrive at the conclusion that the American car is better than the Japanese car requires two short inductive arguments.

Premise: Eighty percent of the people in the sample preferred the American car.

Conclusion: Eighty percent of any group of people would prefer the American car.

Premise: Eighty percent of any group of people would prefer the American car.

Conclusion: The American car is better.

Whether or not you find the second inductive argument convincing, you can see that it depends on the first argument. And how convincing is that one? Consider what that example of inductive reasoning doesn't say. It doesn't tell you how the people were selected for the market research. Were the two hundred people selected at random? If not, then their feelings about the cars will probably be different from the feelings of a different group of two hundred people.

In fact, the people who took part in the market research were carefully chosen. All of them owned American-made cars, so they were more used to the feel and operation of the American car. With this information in mind, the conclusion of the first inductive argument doesn't seem nearly as convincing.

When you're thinking critically about an inductive argument, don't be too quick to take the evidence at face value. Think about the reliability of the evidence and about what might have been left out to make the case sound more convincing.

Activity 23.5

Explain why the premises of the following inductive arguments are too weak to make the conclusions convincing. Discuss your explanations with your classmates.

1. Car X and car Y are the same model with the same features made in the same year. Car X costs $9,500. Car Y must cost $9,500, too.

2. Ella, Raisa, Donna, and Paul took the Test-Rite course, and they scored over 1200 on the Scholastic Aptitude Test. Mariya wants to score over 1200 on the Scholastic Aptitude Test, so she should probably take the Test-Rite course, too.

3. Very special conditions are necessary for living creatures to exist on a planet. Of the nine planets in the solar system, only Earth has the right conditions. In fact, so many things have to be right—temperature, atmosphere, presence of water—that there probably aren't any other planets with life in the entire universe.

4. Pedro and Willy play on the same major league baseball team. Pedro's lifetime batting average is only .247, while Willy's is .313, but Pedro is paid twice as much as Willy is. Pedro must have a better agent than Willy.

5. Felicia was in the last hundred yards of the mile run when she fell down. She still managed to finish third, but she would have won if she hadn't fallen.

6. Val's grade point average is 3.7, while Wayne's is only 2.8, so Val is more likely than Wayne to get into a first-rate college.

7. Here is just some of what audiences said after seeing the movie *Steel Jaw, Clay Feet*: "Spectacular!" "I was on the edge of my seat!" "I never laughed so hard!" You don't want to miss *Steel Jaw, Clay Feet*.

8. Carlyn's cat scratched the legs of the dining room table. Sal's cat chewed the buttons off the couch. Juan's cat ate his parakeet. Cats always make terrible pets.

rethinking
A SUMMARY

Inductive reasoning is the process of using premises to make an inference or draw a conclusion that seems likely or probable. When you think critically about inductive arguments, ask yourself two basic questions.

1. Given the premises, is the conclusion convincing?

2. Are the premises reliable and complete?

If the conclusion is convincing, and if the premises are reliable, then the argument is inductively strong. This doesn't mean, however, that the conclusion is certain. New evidence could appear that would weaken the argument or even change the conclusion.

To practice thinking critically about inductive reasoning, write a critical essay about the following excerpt from an editorial. J. Kay Aldous, the writer of the editorial, believes that Congress should authorize more money for the nation's highways. This belief is not part of an inductive argument, but it is supported by an inductive argument. In your essay, explain how the writer uses inductive reasoning to support his belief. Also, tell how convincing you think his argument is.

As the 102nd Congress turns its attention this year to consideration of a new highway program, the nation's lawmakers ought to bear in mind this recent AAA [American Automobile Association] finding: 94 percent of American motorists think traffic congestion has not improved or has gotten worse in the last year. . . .

The persistent and alarmingly high level of traffic discontent has two principal causes, according to those who daily drive the nation's streets and highways.

First, 69 percent of motorists think inadequate or insufficient roads are the chief cause of deteriorating auto travel conditions.

Second, say a smaller but sizable number of Americans, increasingly difficult travel conditions result from deteriorating roads and bridges. Fifteen percent of motorists believe the condition of roads themselves is a significant cause of traffic delays.

Smaller percentages of the public blame traffic congestion on other factors including driving habits of others, accidents, road construction, and speed limits, AAA found.

Clearly, a significant majority believes an expanded road network in the United States is at least part of the solution to America's traffic woes.

The vast majority of Americans know their traffic future is on the line. Congress needs to approve a long-range highway program that will get America moving well into the next century.

XXIV

DEDUCTION

Suppose that you have never seen a lacewing, but you've been told by a reliable source that it's a kind of insect. You know that all insects have six legs. Now, how many legs does a lacewing have?

The answer is obvious: six. You arrive at this answer by reasoning deductively. If you think about this example of deduction, you'll see that the conclusion is unavoidable. If it's true that lacewings are insects, and true that insects have six legs, then it must be true that lacewings have six legs.

In this chapter, you'll find three ways of reasoning deductively. The first is to use a syllogism, a deductive argument that consists of three parts—two premises and a conclusion.

Later on in the chapter, you'll see how two or more syllogisms can be connected to construct a longer deductive argument.

Finally, you'll see how *if/then* statements (such as *if a car runs out of gasoline, then it won't run*) can be used as the basis of a deductive argument.

syllogisms

Suppose that you have to go to school to register for classes. Everyone has been assigned one of three days to report to school. You don't know which day you're supposed to report, though, so you call the office and talk to one of the secretaries.

She asks you, "What's your name?"

You reply, "Lindstrom."

And she says, "L's register on Tuesday."

Now, whether you're aware of it or not, you and the secretary are using deduction to answer your question. The process of thinking can be described as a syllogism. A syllogism is a deductive argument that states how three terms are related to one another. For instance, in your conversation with the secretary, the three terms are students whose names begin with L, Tuesday registration, and you.

To construct a syllogism, two of these terms must be contained in each of the premises. The two premises would be these:

- All students whose names begin with L should register for classes on Tuesday.

- I am a student whose name begins with L.

The conclusion that you draw from these premises is obvious:

- I am a student who should register for classes on Tuesday.

When a syllogism is properly constructed, the argument is *valid*. This means that if the premises are true, so is the conclusion.

One way to test whether an argument is valid is to use a Venn diagram. This method, devised by English logician John Venn, consists of circles that show whether a conclusion follows logically from the premises.

First, draw two circles to show the relationship between the terms in the first premise. That premise says that all students whose names begin with L are part of the group of students who register on Tuesday.

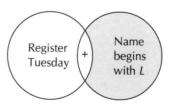

In the diagram, the circle on the left represents students who register on Tuesday. The circle on the right represents students whose names begin with L. Because there are no students whose names begin with L outside the group of students who register on Tuesday, you shade the part of the right-hand circle that doesn't overlap the left-hand circle. The shading shows that that part of the diagram is empty. Then, to show that there *is* someone in the overlapping part of the circles, put a + there.

The second premise says that *you* fall within the group of students whose names begin with L. Therefore, when you add the circle that represents you, it is shaded, except for the part that overlaps the right-hand circle.

For an easy example like this, you don't need a Venn diagram to tell whether the argument is valid. But all arguments aren't this easy. Often, the relationships between the terms in the premises are more complicated. Sometimes, a term represents a group that is excluded from another group. Or, a premise may state that part of a group overlaps part of another group. These more complicated relationships can still be illustrated by Venn diagrams. Here is an example:

Premise: None of the musicians at the party are wearing tuxedos.

Premise: Some of the jugglers are musicians.

Conclusion: Some of the jugglers are not wearing tuxedos.

Is this argument valid? To test it, draw two circles to show the relationship described in the first premise, which says that the group of musicians is entirely separate from the group of people wearing tuxedos. Remember, the shading in the overlapping parts of the circles shows that the two groups do not have members in common.

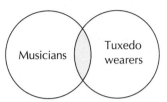

Next, add to the diagram the relationship described in the second premise. In the drawing, a + has been added where the jugglers' circle overlaps the musicians' circle.

Activity 24.1

A Is the argument that some of the jugglers are not wearing tuxedos valid? Do the diagrams prove that some of the jugglers are not wearing tuxedos?

B Suppose the following conclusion was drawn from the same premises. Is it valid?

> Some of the jugglers are wearing tuxedos.

Use the Venn diagram to explain why the conclusion is or is not valid.

C Can more than one valid conclusion be drawn from the same set of premises? Why or why not?

Activity 24.2

Decide whether the following arguments are valid. Draw Venn diagrams to show the relationships. (Remember that even though an argument is valid, its conclusion may be false if it is based on false premises. You don't need to decide whether the premises of these arguments are true, but only whether the conclusions follow from the premises.)

1.   Premise: All tigers have long, sharp teeth.
      Premise: All sharks have long, sharp teeth.
   Conclusion: All tigers are sharks.

2.   Premise: All tigers have long, sharp teeth.
      Premise: Some animals with stripes are tigers.
   Conclusion: Some animals with stripes have long, sharp teeth.

3.   Premise: No generals are English teachers.
      Premise: All English teachers are boring.
   Conclusion: No generals are boring.

4.   Premise: All the students in my physics class want to get an A.
      Premise: Everyone who wants to get an A studies at least three hours every night.
   Conclusion: All the students in my physics class study at least three hours every night.

5.   Premise: Some stockbrokers are crooks.
      Premise: Some crooks are murderers.
   Conclusion: Some stockbrokers are murderers.

6.   Premise: The undercover police officers at the party are dressed like musicians.
      Premise: Some of the undercover police officers are not wearing ties.
   Conclusion: Some of the musicians are not wearing ties.

7.   Premise: No one who wears glasses works as an airline pilot.
      Premise: All nearsighted people wear glasses.
   Conclusion: No nearsighted people work as airline pilots.

8.   Premise: All drivers under the age of twenty-one are speeders.

Premise: Some drivers under the age of twenty-one have taken a course in driver's education.

Conclusion: Some speeders have taken a course in driver's education.

Activity 24.3

The following passage from *Alice's Adventures in Wonderland* by Lewis Carroll contains a deductive argument. Write down the premises and the conclusion of the argument. Then show whether the argument is valid by drawing a Venn diagram.

"But I'm not a serpent, I tell you!" said Alice. "I'm a—I'm a—"

"Well! What are you?" said the Pigeon. "I can see you're trying to invent something!"

"I'm—I'm a little girl," said Alice, rather doubtfully, as she remembered the number of changes she had gone through that day.

"A likely story indeed!" said the Pigeon, in a tone of the deepest contempt. "I've seen a good many little girls in my time, but never *one* with a neck such as that! No, no! You're a serpent; and there's no denying it. I suppose you'll be telling me next that you never tasted an egg!"

"I *have* tasted eggs, certainly," said Alice, who was a very truthful child; "but little girls eat eggs quite as much as serpents do, you know."

"I don't believe it," said the Pigeon; "but if they do, why, then they're a kind of serpent: that's all I can say."

chains of syllogisms

When writers use deductive reasoning, their arguments are often longer than a single syllogism. They may use a number of syllogisms to draw several related conclusions, or they may link together syllogisms by using the conclusion of one as a premise for the next.

Lewis Carroll, who was a logician as well as an author, enjoyed inventing humorous chains of syllogisms. One of them contains the following premises:

Babies are illogical.

No one who can manage a crocodile is despised.

Illogical persons are despised.

To draw a conclusion from these premises, you have to form two syllogisms. The first combines the first and third premises.

Premise: Babies are illogical.

Premise: Illogical persons are despised.

Conclusion: Babies are despised.

The conclusion of this first syllogism can be combined with the remaining premise to create a second syllogism.

Premise: Babies are despised.

Premise: No one who can manage a crocodile is despised.

Conclusion: Babies cannot manage a crocodile.

Carroll's argument is only for fun, of course, but linking syllogisms to construct an argument is often turned to serious purposes. Usually, these arguments are not formally laid out as premises and conclusions, and it isn't always obvious on the first reading that a syllogism is being used.

Activity 24.4

Look for the syllogisms that are implied in the following episode from Arthur Conan Doyle's novel *The Sign of Four*.

In this story, Dr. Watson tries to teach Sherlock Holmes a lesson. Holmes has said that any object a person uses regularly will show signs of the character of the owner. Watson doesn't believe this, and to test Holmes, Watson hands him a pocket watch and asks for an assessment of the character of the watch's owner.

After studying the watch, Holmes complains that he can't tell much, because the watch was cleaned recently. He then says that the watch was owned by Watson's father before it was inherited by Watson's elder brother. As to the character of Watson's elder brother, Holmes concludes:

He was a man of untidy habits—very untidy and careless. He was left with good prospects, but he threw away his chances, lived for some time in poverty with occasional short intervals of prosperity, and finally, taking to drink, he died. That is all I can gather.

On hearing this, Watson becomes angry, insisting that Holmes must have investigated Watson's brother at some time in the past, that Holmes couldn't possibly have learned all that from a brief examination of the watch. Holmes then explains how he reached his deductions.

> When you observe the lower part of that watch case you notice that it is not only dinted in two places but it is cut and marked all over from the habit of keeping other hard objects, such as coins or keys, in the same pocket. Surely it is no great feat to assume that a man who treats a fifty-guinea watch so cavalierly must be a careless man. . . .
>
> It is customary for pawnbrokers in England, when they take a watch, to scratch the numbers of the ticket with a pin-point upon the inside of the case. It is more handy than a label as there is no risk of the number being lost or transposed. There are no less than four such numbers visible to my lens on the inside of this case. Inference—that your brother was often at low water. Secondary inference—that he had occasional bursts of prosperity, or he could not have redeemed the pledge. Finally, I ask you to look at the inner plate, which contains the keyhole. Look at the thousands of scratches all round the hole— marks where the key has slipped. What sober man's key could have scorched those grooves? But you will never see a drunkard's watch without them. He winds it at night, and he leaves these traces of his unsteady hand. Where is the mystery in all this?

A Write the premises that lead to Holmes's conclusion that the owner of the watch was careless.

B Write the premises that lead to Holmes's second conclusion: The owner of the watch often needed money. (Hint: This argument contains two linking syllogisms.)

C Write the premises that lead to Holmes's third conclusion: The owner of the watch was a drunkard.

D Are Holmes's arguments valid or invalid? Do you accept his premises as true? Why or why not?

Activity 24.5

The following premises are from another one of Lewis Carroll's linking syllogisms. What conclusion can you validly draw from these premises? (Hint: If you arrive at a valid conclusion, you will be able to say whether wedding cake agrees with Carroll.)

- The only articles of food that my doctor allows me are such as are not very rich.
- Nothing that agrees with me is unsuitable for supper.
- Wedding cake is always very rich.
- My doctor allows me all articles of food that are suitable for supper.

if . . . then . . .

Suppose you have a little brother who wanders around the house, looking for someone to play a game with. Everyone is either too busy or not interested, and finally the little boy complains, "If nobody wants to play a game with me, that means nobody likes me."

Now, your little brother probably isn't aware of it, but he's using deductive reasoning. He stated only one premise of the argument, but the rest is pretty clear.

Premise: If nobody wants to play a game with me, then nobody likes me.

Premise: Nobody wants to play a game with me.

Conclusion: Nobody likes me.

This is a valid deductive argument. If the premises are true, then the conclusion must be true also. (You may think that the first premise is false, but that question is different from deciding whether the argument is valid.)

There are two ways to draw a valid conclusion in an argument that begins with an *if/then* premise. The first way has already been shown. You state in the second premise that the *if* part of the first premise is true. It follows that the *then* part of the first premise must be true also.

The second way of drawing a valid conclusion from an *if/then* premise is to state in the second premise that the *then* part of the first premise is false. In that case, you can validly conclude that the *if* part of the first premise is also false. An example of this kind of reasoning was given by some people who were watching the movie *Raiders of the Lost Ark*. They noted that in the opening scene Indiana Jones grabs what is supposed to be a solid gold idol, swinging and throwing it with ease. After some computation, they figured that if an idol that size were really solid gold, it would weigh about forty pounds, and they concluded that the idol must not have been solid gold. If you express these ideas in terms of premises and a conclusion, you come up with the following valid argument.

Premise: If the idol were solid gold, then it would be heavy to carry.

Premise: It isn't heavy to carry.

Conclusion: The idol is not solid gold.

Activity 24.6

A lawyer, a doctor, and a blind philosopher were competing to prove who was the best thinker. Their final test involved five stickers—two red and three blue. The person judging the contest put one sticker on the back of each contestant, but without telling them what color the sticker was. The contestants were then challenged to say what color sticker they were wearing. A contestant who guessed correctly would win; one who guessed incorrectly would be disqualified. The lawyer looked at the backs of the other two and then shook his head; he couldn't make a guess. The doctor looked at the sticker on the lawyer's back and at the one on the philosopher's back; she considered the lawyer's inability to make a guess; finally, she, too, decided not to make a guess. The blind philosopher immediately announced what color sticker she was wearing and explained by deductive reasoning how she knew. Write out the philosopher's reasoning in the form of premises and conclusions. (Hint: You will need two arguments, each consisting of two premises and a conclusion. The first premise in each argument should be an *if/then* statement.)

Activity 24.7

In a dialogue recorded by the ancient Greek philosopher Plato, he tells how Socrates and Meno tried to decide whether virtue can be taught. Socrates says that for everything that can be taught there are teachers. Meno agrees with this, so Socrates goes on to say that if anyone could teach virtue, then certainly the Sophists (well-known teachers of the time) or the noblest Athenians would do it. Meno goes along with this also. But look at the facts, says Socrates: Among the students of the Sophists and the sons of the noble Athenians are many who were not virtuous. Those teachers and parents would certainly have taught virtue if they could have. Therefore, says Socrates, we must conclude that virtue cannot be taught.

Write out Socrates' argument in the form of premises and a conclusion. (Hint: You may put more than one *if/then* premise in the argument.) Is the argument valid? Do you find the argument convincing? Why or why not?

Activity 24.8

A Tell whether the following arguments are valid or invalid. Explain your answers. (Hint: Think of a way that the premises would be true but the conclusion would be false.)

1. If a car runs out of gasoline, it won't run.
   Our car isn't running.
   Therefore, our car is out of gasoline.
2. If a car runs out of gasoline, it won't run.
   Our car has gasoline.
   Therefore, our car runs.
3. If a baby has a dirty diaper, the baby cries.
   Our baby is crying.
   Therefore, our baby has a dirty diaper.
4. If a teacher is mean, she assigns a lot of homework.
   Our teacher isn't mean.
   Therefore, our teacher doesn't assign a lot of homework.

B What do the examples in A show about *if/then* deductive arguments? (Hint: Can you draw a valid conclusion when the *then* part of the first premise is true? How about when the *if* part of the first premise is false?)

rethinking

A   SUMMARY

Deductive reasoning is the process of using evidence or premises to show that a conclusion must necessarily be true.

The traditional form of deductive reasoning is the syllogism, which states in two premises how three terms are related to one another. If the argument is properly constructed, there will be one valid conclusion that can be drawn. The fact that the conclusion is *valid* means that if the premises are true, the conclusion must be true also.

A deductive argument can also be constructed from several syllogisms. These might be used independently to make related points, or they can be combined to lead to an ultimate conclusion by turning the conclusion of one syllogism into a premise of the next syllogism.

In addition, deductive arguments can be based on *if/then* statements (such as *if the temperature of water under normal pressure exceeds 100° Celsius, then the water will boil*). This statement would be the first premise of the argument. If the second premise stated either that the *if* part of the first premise was true *or* that the *then* part of the first premise was false, a valid conclusion could be drawn.

To practice thinking critically about deductive reasoning, write an essay that analyzes and evaluates the argument made in the following Supreme Court decision. Your essay should explain the deductive argument used by the justices as well as tell whether the argument is valid and whether you find it convincing.

In the 1920s a fifty-year-old woman applied for citizenship in the United States. In her application, she said that she was a pacifist and would refuse to fight to defend the country. Because the law said that naturalized citizens had to be willing to "support and defend the Constitution and the laws of the United States against all enemies," she was denied citizenship. She appealed this decision, and when her case reached the Supreme Court, six of the nine justices ruled that she should not be allowed to become a citizen. They argued that if every citizen believed as she did, the Constitution and the government would cease to exist. The facts that she was a woman and too old to serve in the armed forces didn't matter, said the justices. The influence of the views of people like her was "apt to be more detrimental than their mere refusal to bear arms." The justices felt that in a time of war, she would be a "menace to the country."

XXV

NONSENSE

I t's not always easy to tell when an argument makes sense. Sometimes nonsense is dressed up to look reasonable. Take, for example, the following syllogism:

Premise: An English teacher from City High was on television last night.

Premise: Ms. Fernandez is an English teacher from City High.

Conclusion: Ms. Fernandez was on television last night.

You probably aren't going to be fooled by an argument like that. In fact, you might think of it as a joke, not an attempt to trick you. But sometimes, nonsense does trick people. This chapter is about three kinds of deceptive nonsense.

The first is the result of information presented in an unclear or distorted manner. If an argument uses vague or ambiguous terms, it can create a false impression. The argument seems to be talking about one thing, but in fact is talking about something else. This is what's wrong with the syllogism above. In the first premise, the phrase "an English teacher from City High" refers to a particular individual. But in the second premise, the same words are used to stand for a group of people. The syllogism is nonsensical because this phrase is ambiguous.

The second kind of nonsense discussed in the chapter occurs when an argument is presented without all its premises. Leaving a weak premise unstated can make an argument seem stronger than it really is.

The third kind of nonsense is usually called "begging the question." The conclusion that is supposed to be proved is simply assumed.

false impressions

Sometimes, information is represented in a way that seems to mean one thing but, on closer examination, turns out to mean something different. For instance, Graph 1 shows the average scores of four English classes on an achievement test. Pretty big difference between class A and the other three—right?

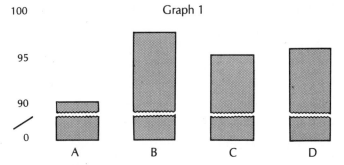

Or is there? Graph 2 shows the same information, but here the bars are shown full length instead of cut short as was done in Graph 1. In Graph 2, the four classes look about equal.

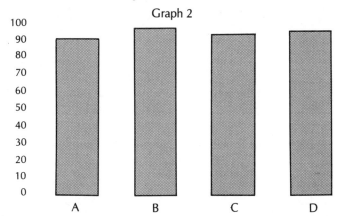

There's nothing in Graph 1 that says, "Class A did much worse than the other three classes." But the information is presented in a way that encourages that impression.

Just as statistics can be presented in ways that might lead you to draw an unjustified conclusion, so, too, language can be used to create false impressions. Suppose, for example, that you see a television commercial urging you to call a 900 number so "you can talk to an actual psychic!"

Before you rush to the phone, ask yourself what you expect to get for the cost of the call. What exactly is an "actual psychic"? Are psychics licensed or certified like doctors and teachers? Or can anyone claim to be a psychic? What does a psychic do?

Once you begin to think about questions like these, you'll find that the meaning of the ad is different from the impression it gives at first.

Activity 25.1

What impression does each of the following advertising claims give at first? How is the meaning of the claim different from that first impression? (Hint: Think about the vague word or phrase in each claim.)

1. "It isn't just ice cream! It's Gregg's Great Ice Cream!"

2. "With this new exercise videotape, you can get a ninety-minute workout in just thirty minutes."

3. "Our dog and cat foods have been developed by veterinarians to provide a scientific diet for your pet."

4. "Power windows, power door locks, reclining seats! Anti-lock brakes! And you get all that for *under* eighteen thousand dollars!" (The car costs $17,900.)

5. A commercial for a men's hair care product shows a middle-aged man whose problem is "gray, thinning hair." The product is supposed to cure the problem in two ways: it colors hair and thickens it. Photos of a hair before and after treatment show how the hair has become darker and thicker. (Hint: What does "thinning hair" mean? What do the before-and-after photos imply that "thinning hair" means?)

Activity 25.2

The following information describes a projected increase in electric rates. Who do you think sent out this information—the electric company asking for the increase or the consumer group opposing it? (Hint: Is the information presented in a way that makes the increase seem large or small? Can you easily see by about how much an average monthly bill would go up? What impression is created by the detailed precision of the figures about the increase? Why is this precision a bit silly? Can you tell how the figures were computed?)

Monthly Current Average Bill	Proposed Annual Increase	Percent Increase	5-Year Projected Increase
$ 20	$ 38.50	16.04	$ 192.50
30	54.91	15.25	274.56
40	71.32	14.86	356.61
50	87.73	14.62	438.66
60	149.22	20.73	746.30
70	199.22	23.72	996.11
80	204.45	21.30	1,022.25
90	209.68	19.42	1,048.39
100	214.91	17.91	1,074.55

Activity 25.3

The following argument was devised by Jerry Cederblom and David W. Paulsen to show how deductions based on vague terms can be misleading. Explain why the argument is not really valid. (Hint: Think about what *compatible* means in the second and third premises.)

1. Getting married involves promising to live with a person for the rest of one's life.

2. No one can safely predict compatibility with another person for life.

3. If two people aren't compatible, then they can't live together.

4. No one should make a promise unless she or he can safely predict that she or he can keep it.

   Therefore, no one should get married.

Activity 25.4

What's wrong with the following argument? (Hint: The argument seems to be explaining the cause of a number of problems. Does it really explain them?)

Studies have shown that nearly one hundred percent of all criminals drank milk as children. This is even true of those who have committed violent crimes. The occasional drinking of milk by street gang members has been estimated at over 96 percent. Nearly 97.3 percent of hard-core gamblers have confessed to bouts of milk drinking. Moreover, the evil effects of milk not only warp people's attitudes and sap their moral fiber but also lead to inevitable physical debilitation. Professional athletes who have continued their milk-drinking past the age of forty have found their reflexes slower, their speed reduced, their strength diminished. Most importantly, the effects of milk drinking are not reversible. Exhaustive research has failed to discover even one milk-drinker born prior to 1880 who is still alive. All the rest have perished. We must take action against this scourge today.

missing premises

With the premises of an argument fully stated, you can see whether the argument is valid, and you can also see whether you believe the premises to be true. Because it is easy to see through weak arguments that are stated fully and clearly, people sometimes present weak arguments with some of the premises missing. This can make the argument *appear* stronger, and if you don't examine the argument carefully, you can be misled.

For example, the advertisements for a brand of ketchup offered evidence that their brand was thicker than "any other leading brand." this premise—"our brand is thicker than any other leading brand"—was the basis for the conclusion—"you should buy our brand."

For this argument to be valid, there obviously has to be another premise—something like "you want to buy thick ketchup." But even with that vague premise added, you still would not have a valid argument, because there may be a dozen *nonleading* brands of ketchup that are thicker than the advertised brand. To make the argument valid, another premise is needed, one that says either that the advertised brand is exactly as thick as you want it or that you only buy "leading brands."

So it would be possible to make the argument in the ketchup commercial valid. But if it was made valid, it would come out something like this:

Premise: You want to buy thick ketchup.

Premise: You only buy leading brands.

Premise: Our brand is thicker than any other leading brand.

Conclusion: You should buy our brand.

Although this argument is valid, it isn't very persuasive. Once the first two premises are clearly stated, you can easily see that they're probably false. And if they're false, then the conclusion is false, too.

Activity 25.5

The ketchup commercial does not have to be thought of as an attempt to make a valid *deductive* argument. It might be considered instead to be an *inductive* argument. In that case, the premises would only have to make the conclusion seem likely, not certain. The stated premise of this inductive argument would still be

Our brand is thicker than any other leading brand.

What would the second premise of the argument be? (Hint: The premise will have to make a claim about how "thickness" affects the quality of ketchup.) How convincing is this argument? Is it any more persuasive than the deductive argument? Why or why not?

Activity 25.6

Each of the following arguments is missing a premise needed to make the argument valid. Write out the arguments by filling in the missing premises. Then tell whether you find the fully stated argument convincing.

1. A commercial for a gasoline company contains the following premises:

   • You are what you eat.
   • What's true of a man is true of machines.

The conclusion drawn is that you should buy their brand of gasoline. (Hint: You'll have to revise the first two premises to make them clearer. For instance, the first premise could be phrased like this:

To have a lot of energy, you need to eat high-energy food.

Even after you restate the first two premises, you'll still need to add two more premises to complete the argument.)

2. A commercial for a long-distance phone company urges people to use its service, because "The longer you talk, the more you save."

3. In a political ad, a woman running for the office of state's attorney was criticized by her opponent. According to the opponent, when this women worked in the state's attorney's office, she got convictions in only forty-seven percent of the drug cases she prosecuted. Therefore, the ad concluded, the woman was not an effective prosecutor.

4. "Cola Light! Only one calorie per bottle!"

5. A television commercial for a car shows a man driving the car very fast along a curving highway on which there are no other cars.

6. A television commercial for a breath mint shows people avoiding an attractive woman. Then she chews the breath mint. In the next scene, the people who had avoided her are eager to be close to her.

Activity 25.7

Find an ad that uses an argument with a missing premise. You can take the ad from television, radio, a newspaper, or a magazine. Write down the ad as it is presented. Then write what the argument would be if it were made valid by stating it fully. Share your work with your classmates, and explain whether the fully stated argument would make the ad more or less persuasive.

begging the question

Some gang members are trying to decide on their next crime. Finally, one of them says, "Look, we're going to do what I say!"

"How come you get to decide?" a second one asks.

"Because I'm the boss," says the first one.

"And what makes you the boss?"

"Because I'm the one who makes the decisions."

The gang members may have found this argument convincing, but chances are you can see there's something wrong with it. The argument goes in a circle. First the boss uses the premise that he *is* the boss to prove that he should make the decisions; then he uses the premise that he makes the decisions to prove that he is the boss.

This kind of argument begs the questions. When you beg the question, you assume as true the point you're trying to prove.

Advertisers often beg the question by assuming that their product is the best of its kind or that you want to buy it. For instance, the selling point in a series of television commercials for an expensive American car was that the car cost much less than some European luxury cars. What the commercials assumed was that the American car was as well engineered as the European cars. But this assumption was exactly the point the commercials were trying to prove.

To recognize instances of begging the question, be on the lookout for arguments that move in a circle and for arguments in which the conclusion is smuggled into the premises.

Activity 25.8

Explain why each of the following is an example of begging the question.

1. A man and a woman are talking about the woman getting the muffler fixed on her car.

    "Did you go to the discount muffler place?" the man asks.

    "No," says the woman, "I went to Muffler City. I felt quality was just as important as price."

2. A woman is shown eating a cracker. "A lot of you," she says into the camera, "are eating Oat Fiber Crunchies because they taste good. If you eat them because they taste good, you're missing the point." (Hint: Why do people eat snack crackers?)

3. Two women are talking about the first woman's business successes and about the new car she has bought to celebrate. The car is the same model of car she had owned before.

    "I thought," says the second woman with a knowing grin, "that you were going to *move up*. How will people know how successful you are?"

4. "If you want the lowest prices, it's always better to shop at Al's."

5. The following is from *The Little Prince*, the story of an unusual prince who travels through space, visiting strange planets.

    The next planet was inhabited by a tippler [alcoholic]. This was a very short visit, but it plunged the little prince into deep dejection.

    "What are you doing there?" he said to the tippler, whom he found settled down in silence before a collection of empty bottles and also a collection of full bottles.

"I am drinking," replied the tippler, with a lugubrious air.

"Why are you drinking?" demanded the little prince.

"So that I may forget," replied the tippler.

"Forget what?" inquired the little prince, who already was sorry for him.

"Forget that I am ashamed," the tippler confessed, hanging his head.

"Ashamed of what?" insisted the little prince, who wanted to help him.

"Ashamed of drinking!" The tippler brought his speech to an end, and shut himself up in an impregnable silence.

And the little prince went away, puzzled.

"The grown-ups are certainly very, very odd," he said to himself, as he continued on his journey.

—ANTOINE DE SAINT-EXUPÉRY
(trans. Katherine Woods)

6. Two students engage in a dialogue about women and politics.

HAL: A woman could never be elected President of the United States.

ERIN: I don't see why not. There's no law against it.

HAL: But people wouldn't vote for her.

ERIN: I would.

HAL: But most people wouldn't. People want their vote to count: they want to vote for a winner. Everybody knows that a woman would lose, so they wouldn't vote for her.

rethinking
A   S U M M A R Y

In this chapter, you've seen three kinds of nonsense, three ways that arguments can be deceptive.

Sometimes an argument is nonsensical because it's based on ambiguity or distortion. It creates a false impression by using two meanings of a word without distinguishing them or by presenting evidence in a deceptive way. The result is that the argument is not really saying what it seems to be saying.

An argument can also become nonsensical when it's presented without all its premises being stated. If you think about the premises that are unsaid, you may find that the conclusion is questionable.

Finally, an argument is nonsensical if it begs the question by assuming as true what it's supposed to prove.

You can practice thinking critically about nonsense by writing an essay using the following excerpt from a speech given by Adolf Hitler in 1934. Hitler was the dictator of Germany from 1933 to 1945. In your essay, you can discuss Hitler's vague and ambiguous language, his incomplete arguments, or his begging of the question. Whatever you focus on, the aim of your essay should be to show how what might at first sound reasonable is, in fact, nonsense.

In this speech, Hitler defended the recent killings of hundreds of German citizens, claiming that those who died had been plotting against him and against the nation. Many Germans felt that trials should have been held. But Hitler argued that judicial procedures were not necessary.

> If people bring against me the objection that only a judicial procedure could precisely weigh the measure of the guilt and of its expiation, then against this view I lodge my most solemn protest. He who rises against Germany is a traitor to his country: and the traitor to his country is not to be punished according to the range and the extent of his act, but according to the purpose that that act has revealed. He who in his heart purposes to raise a mutiny and thereby breaks loyalty, breaks faith, breaks sacred pledges, he can expect nothing else than that he himself will be the first sacrifice. I have no intention to have the little culprits shot and to spare the great criminals. It is not my duty to inquire whether it was too hard a lot that was inflicted on these conspirators, these agitators and destroyers, these poisoners of the wellsprings of German public opinion and in a wider sense of world opinion: it is not mine to consider which of them suffered too severely: I have only to see to it that Germany's lot should not be intolerable.

XXVI

EVALUATING

English historian George Macaulay Trevelyan wrote, "Education . . . has produced a vast population able to read but unable to distinguish what is worth reading." He may have exaggerated the condition of education, but he was right about the difference between recognizing groups of letters on a page and knowing what to make of them. You begin to think critically by figuring out the meaning of what you see and hear. You continue the process by deciding whether what you see and hear makes sense. But the process doesn't end there.

If you suppose that critical thinking is simply a matter of figuring out the meanings of words and deciding whether they make sense, then the process will seem like arranging furniture. You try to organize ideas so that they fit together neatly. But critical thinking isn't really like that. It isn't something that goes on outside you. The way you arrange ideas in your mind changes you. After you decide that something is true or good or beautiful, you aren't the same person anymore.

In other words, critical thinking leads to evaluating. For example, having decided what the words in a poem mean and whether they make sense, you go on to think about what the poem means *to you*. Is it worth memorizing? Do you want to share it with a friend? Does it capture a feeling that you have felt? Is it funny? Is it sad? Do the ideas inspire you? Is the language musical? Did the poet understand what she or he was talking about? Did you find yourself thinking about the poem after you'd read it? Would you like to read another poem like this one? Does the poem raise questions for you? Does the poem have answers? Is it dramatic? Is it cold? Is it lively? Is it true?

When you evaluate, you think reflectively, creatively, critically. You bring all your experience to bear on the object of your thoughts. The questions you ask take many forms, but all of them boil down to this one: "What does it mean *to me?*"

Activity 26.1

Suppose that you are the editor of a poetry anthology for high school students. The two poems that follow have both been suggested, but there's room for only one in your book. Which one should be included? Why? Write a memo to your publisher explaining your choice.

> How do I love thee? Let me count the ways.
> I love thee to the depth and breadth and height
> My soul can reach, when feeling out of sight
> For the ends of Being and ideal Grace.
> I love thee to the level of everyday's
> Most quiet need, by sun and candle light.
> I love thee freely, as men strive for Right;
> I love thee purely, as they turn from Praise.
> I love thee with the passion put to use
> In my old griefs, and with my childhood's faith.
> I love thee with a love I seemed to lose
> With my lost saints—I love thee with the breath,
> Smiles, tears, of all my life—and, if God choose,
> I shall but love thee better after death.
>
> —ELIZABETH BARRETT BROWNING

*   *   *   *

> I died for beauty, but was scarce
> Adjusted in the tomb,
> When one who died for truth was lain
> In an adjoining room.
>
> He questioned softly why I failed?
> "For beauty," I replied.
> "And I for truth,—the two are one;
> We brethren are," he said.

And so, as kinsmen met a night,
We talked between the rooms,
Until the moss had reached our lips,
And covered up our names.

—EMILY DICKINSON

Activity 26.2

Suppose that another unmanned rocket is being sent to explore deep space. Like the *Voyagers*, it will contain numerous artifacts to show any who might find it what life on Earth is like. Among the artifacts will be a tape recording of music from around the world—classical, folk, and popular. Write a letter in which you nominate a piece of music to be included. In your letter, explain and defend your choice.

Activity 26.3

The following speech comes from a dialogue by Irish writer Oscar Wilde. The speaker is a man named Vivian. Write a character sketch of Vivian. Is Vivian someone you would like to have as a friend? Why or why not? Include your answers to these questions in your character sketch.

It is a humiliating confession, but we are all of us made out of the same stuff. In Falstaff there is something of Hamlet, in Hamlet there is not a little of Falstaff. The fat knight has his moods of melancholy, and the young prince his moments of coarse humor. Where we differ from each other is purely in accidentals: in personal appearance, tricks of habit, and the like. The more one analyzes people, the more all reasons for analysis disappear. Sooner or later one comes to that dreadful universal thing called human nature. Indeed, as anyone who has ever worked among the poor knows only too well, the brotherhood of man is no mere poet's dream, it is a most depressing and humiliating reality; and if a writer insists upon analyzing the upper classes, he might just as well write of match-girls and costermongers [street peddlars] at once.

Activity 26.4

Imagine you're an official of a worldwide health organization, seeking people to work with some remote tribes in South America and Australia. You want to hire people who will sympathize with as well as understand the tribes. Assume that the following statement expresses the views of one applicant for the job. Do you think this person should be hired? Why or why not? Write a brief letter to the applicant explaining why you are or are not recommending him.

> Led astray by his ignorance of the true cause of things, primitive man believed that in order to produce the great phenomena of nature on which his life depended he had only to imitate them, and that immediately by a secret sympathy or mystic influence the little drama which he acted in a forest glade or mountain dell, on desert plain or windswept shore, would be taken up and repeated by mightier actors on a vaster stage. He fancied that by masquerading in leaves and flowers he helped the bare earth to clothe herself with verdure [fresh greenness], and that by playing the death and burial of winter he drove the gloomy season away, and made smooth the path for the footsteps of returning spring. If we find it hard to throw ourselves even in fancy into a mental condition in which such things seem possible, we can more easily picture to ourselves the anxiety which the savage, when he first began to lift his thoughts above the satisfaction of his merely animal wants, and to meditate on the causes of things, may have felt as to the continued operation of what we now call the laws of nature. To us, familiar as we are with the conception of the uniformity and regularity with which the great cosmic phenomena succeed each other, there seems little ground for apprehension that the causes which produce these effects will cease to operate, at least within the near future. But this confidence in the stability of nature is bred only by the experience which comes of wide observation and long tradition; and the savage, with his narrow sphere of observation and his short-lived tradition, lacks the very elements of that experience which alone could set his mind at rest in face of the ever-changing and often menacing aspects of nature. No wonder, therefore, that he is thrown into a panic by an eclipse, and thinks that the sun or the moon would surely perish, if he did not raise a clamor and shoot his puny shafts into the air to defend the luminaries from the monster who threatens to devour them.
>
> —SIR JAMES GEORGE FRAZER

Activity 26.5

Suppose that you are a history teacher on a committee to decide what books will be read in a world history course. Two members of the committee want to include a few selections from the work of the ancient Roman historian Tacitus. Two others feel that Tacitus won't be interesting or relevant to today's high school students. Judging by the following excerpt from Tacitus's *Annals*, what do you think? Should Tacitus be included? Why or why not? Write a brief statement of your view.

> But all human efforts, all the lavish gifts of the emperor [Nero], and the propitiations of the gods, did not banish the sinister belief that the conflagration [the burning of Rome] was the result of an order [given by Nero]. Consequently, to get rid of the report, Nero fastened the guilt and inflicted the most exquisite tortures on a class hated for their abominations, called Christians by the populace. Christus, from whom the name had its origin, suffered the extreme penalty during the reign of Tiberius at the hands of one of our procurators, Pontius Pilatus, and a most michievous superstition, thus checked for the moment, again broke out not in Judea, the first source of the evil, but even in Rome, where all things hideous and shameful from every part of the world find their center and become popular. Accordingly, an arrest was first made of all who pleaded guilty; then, upon their information, an immense multitude was convicted, not so much of the crime of firing the city, as of hatred against mankind. Mockery of every sort was added to their deaths. Covered with the skins of beasts, they were torn by dogs and perished, or were nailed to crosses, or were doomed to the flames and burnt, to serve as a nightly illumination, when daylight had expired.
>
> Nero offered his gardens for the spectacle, and was exhibiting a show in the circus, while he mingled with the people in the dress of a charioteer or stood aloft on a car [chariot]. Hence, even for criminals who deserved extreme and exemplary punishment, there arose a feeling of compassion; for it was not, as it seemed, for the public good, but to glut one man's cruelty, that they were being destroyed.
>
> —trans. ALFRED JOHN CHURCH
> and WILLIAM JACKSON BRODRIBB

Activity 26.6

The two excerpts that follow are from an essay about humor by Canadian professor and humorist Stephen Leacock. Which excerpt do you think does a better job of getting at what is really important about humor? Why? What do you learn about humor from that excerpt? Reply to these questions in an essay of your own.

I

Any man will admit, if need be, that his sight is not good, or that he cannot swim, or shoots badly with a rifle, but to touch upon his sense of humor is to give him a mortal affront.

"No," said a friend of mine the other day, "I never go to Grand Opera," and then he added with an air of pride—"You see, I have absolutely no ear for music."

"You don't say so!" I exclaimed.

"None!" he went on. "I can't tell one tune from another. I don't know *Home, Sweet Home* from *God Save the King*. I can't tell whether a man is tuning a violin or playing a sonata."

He seemed to get prouder and prouder over each item of his own deficiency. He ended by saying that he had a dog at his house that had a far better ear for music than he had. As soon as his wife or any visitor started to play the piano the dog always began to howl—plaintively, he said, as if it were hurt. He himself never did this.

When he had finished I made what I thought a harmless comment.

"I suppose," I said, "that you find your sense of humor deficient in the same way: the two generally go together."

My friend was livid with rage in a moment.

"Sense of humor!" he said. "My sense of humor! Me without a sense of humor! Why, I suppose I've a keener sense of humor than any man, or any two men, in this city!"

From that he turned to bitter personal attack.

He said that my sense of humor seemed to have withered altogether.

He left me, still quivering with indignation.

II

The deep background that lies behind and beyond what we call humor is revealed only to the few who, by instinct or by effort, have given thought to it. The world's humor, in its best and greatest sense, is perhaps the highest product of our civilization. . . . Its basis lies in the deeper contrasts offered by life itself: the strange incongruity between our aspiration and our achievement, the eager and fretful anxieties of today that fade into nothingness tomorrow, the burning pain and the sharp sorrow that are softened in the gentle retrospect of time, till as we look back upon the course that has been traversed, we pass in view the panorama of our lives, as people in old age may recall, with mingled tears and smiles, the angry quarrels of their childhood. And here, in its larger aspect, humor is blended with pathos till the two are one, and represent, as they have in every age, the mingled heritage of tears and laughter that is our lot on earth.

INDEX

Answer Key

Activity 2.1 (quiz), pages 13–15

Remember, as you score this quiz, you are to check only those answers that the quiz-taker is *positive* are correct. The point of the quiz is not to find out how many of these questions you can answer. The point is to find out whether you can tell what you really know. Anyone who can tell what he or she knows will get a perfect score.

Don't be surprised if it turns out you are mistaken about some of the things you were sure of. Everyone says, now and then, "Hey, I didn't know that!" Let the quiz be a reminder that you need to ask yourself, "How do I know that? What makes me so certain?"

1. False. Only slaves in Confederate territories were freed.

2. Three cats will be needed.

3. True. Tornadoes spin counterclockwise in the Northern Hemisphere and clockwise in the Southern Hemisphere.

4. Franklin Roosevelt, Harry S. Truman, Dwight D. Eisenhower, John F. Kennedy, Lyndon B. Johnson, Richard M. Nixon, Gerald Ford, Jimmy Carter, Ronald Reagan, George Bush.

5. In the corner

6. 1969

7. A viola

8. William Shakespeare

9. False. The backward expulsion of gas produces the forward thrust. The engine is based on Newton's third law of motion.

10. 13 cards

11. 12 checkers

12. $365\frac{1}{4}$ days

13. Nursing

14. Alaska

15. 7

16. False. The odds are still 50:50.

17. 212 degrees Fahrenheit (100 degrees Celsius).

18. Sand

19. True

20. Egypt

21. If you count a centerfielder as a center, then all four types of teams have a center; otherwise, all but baseball.

22. Probably false, but neither answer can be entirely certain, because the evidence about dinosaurs is not definite.

23. The bicycle

24. Only one—Lake Michigan

25. Benjamin Franklin proved that lightning is electricity.

26. It takes thunder longer to travel two miles than it takes the light of the sun to travel to Earth.

27. She does not really want to know anything; she is wishing that he was not a Montague (the family that is the enemy of her family), so she asks why he must be named Romeo Montague, instead of being of some other family.

28. Elvis Presley

29. One—the Eighteenth Amendment (Prohibition).

30. It is a theory, or scientific model, that predicts that the buildup of carbon dioxide in the atmosphere will cause average temperatures on Earth to increase enough to melt the polar ice caps and alter climate patterns.

Quiz Answers for Ch. 5, page 45–46 (Illusions)

1. There are 17 *f*s in the sentence. Many people miss the *f*s in the word *of*.

2. The lines are the same length.

3. The trick is that the word *the* appears both at the end of the fourth line and at the beginning of the fifth line; readers tend to see only one "the" when they read the poem aloud.

4. Both arrows are equally bright. The background makes them appear different.

5. The people are standing in a trick room. The man and the woman are about the same height.

6. A and B are parallel to one another.

7. Segments A and B would make a straight line.

Answer photo for Activity 5.1, part D, page 48:

About the Author

Robert Boostrom is a Visiting Scholar at the University of Chicago's Benton Center for Curriculum and Instruction, where he received his Ph.D. As a graduate student, he pursued his interests in thinking by studying both philosophy and education. He is currently working with Philip W. Jackson of the University of Chicago and David T. Hansen of the University of Illinois at Chicago on a book about the moral life of schools. This book and Boostrom's other writings about the moral significance of classroom rules are based on two years of classroom observations in a variety of urban schools.

Prior to becoming an educational researcher, Boostrom was a textbook editor, specializing in the field of English composition. He also worked as a free-lance writer, contributing to a number of high school English texts. In these, he has written about composition and literature, as well as about creative and critical thinking.

Boostrom was a high school teacher for five years. He taught American history, anthropology, English literature and composition, and reading. He also coordinated the reading program at a magnet high school that focuses on the health professions, where he drew upon the vocational interests of the students to make their reading more reflective, thoughtful, and meaningful. In addition, he served on a committee that composed curriculum and test materials used throughout the Dallas Independent School District.

Boostrom acknowledges that most of what he knows about the development of thinking he learned by watching his sons—Rob, Adam, and Alex.

NTC LANGUAGE ARTS BOOKS

Business Communication
Handbook for Business Writing, *Baugh, Fryar, & Thomas*
Meetings: Rules & Procedures, *Pohl*

Dictionaries
British/American Language Dictionary, *Moss*
NTC's Classical Dictionary, *Room*
NTC's Dictionary of Changes in Meaning, *Room*
NTC's Dictionary of Debate, *Hanson*
NTC's Dictionary of Literary Terms, *Morner & Rausch*
NTC's Dictionary of Theatre and Drama Terms, *Mobley*
NTC's Dictionary of Word Origins, *Room*
NTC's Spell It Right Dictionary, *Downing*
Robin Hyman's Dictionary of Quotations

Essential Skills
Building Real Life English Skills, *Starkey & Penn*
Developing Creative & Critical Thinking, *Boostrom*
English Survival Series, *Maggs*
Essential Life Skills, *Starkey & Penn*
Essentials of English Grammar, *Baugh*
Essentials of Reading and Writing English Series
Grammar for Use, *Hall*
Grammar Step-by-Step, *Pratt*
Guide to Better English Spelling, *Furness*
How to Be a Rapid Reader, *Redway*
How to Improve Your Study Skills, *Coman & Heavers*
How to Write Term Papers and Reports, *Baugh*
NTC Skill Builders
Reading by Doing, *Simmons & Palmer*
303 Dumb Spelling Mistakes, *Downing*
TIME: We the People, *ed. Schinke-Llano*
Vocabulary by Doing, *Beckert*

Genre Literature
Coming of Age, *Emra*
The Detective Story, *Schwartz*
The Short Story & You, *Simmons & Stern*
Sports in Literature, *Emra*
You and Science Fiction, *Hollister*

Journalism
Getting Started in Journalism, *Harkrider*
Journalism Today! *Ferguson & Patten*
Publishing the Literary Magazine, *Klaiman*
UPI Stylebook, *United Press International*

Language, Literature, and Composition
African American Literature, *Worley & Perry*
An Anthology for Young Writers, *Meredith*
The Art of Composition, *Meredith*
Creative Writing, *Mueller & Reynolds*
Handbook for Practical Letter Writing, *Baugh*
How to Write Term Papers and Reports, *Baugh*

In a New Land, *Grossman & Schur*
Literature by Doing, *Tchudi & Yesner*
Lively Writing, *Schrank*
Look, Think & Write, *Leavitt & Sohn*
NTC Shakespeare Series
NTC Vocabulary Builders
Poetry by Doing, *Osborn*
World Literature, *Rosenberg*
Write to the Point! *Morgan*
The Writer's Handbook, *Karls & Szymanski*
Writing by Doing, *Sohn & Enger*
Writing in Action, *Meredith*

Media Communication
Getting Started in Mass Media, *Beckert*
Photography in Focus, *Jacobs & Kokrda*
Television Production Today!, *Bielak*
Understanding Mass Media, *Schrank*
Understanding the Film, *Bone & Johnson*

Mythology
The Ancient World, *Sawyer & Townsend*
Mythology and You, *Rosenberg & Baker*
Welcome to Ancient Greece, *Millard*
Welcome to Ancient Rome, *Millard*
World Mythology, *Rosenberg*

Speech
Activities for Effective Communication, *LiSacchi*
The Basics of Speech, *Galvin, Cooper, & Gordon*
Contemporary Speech, *HopKins & Whitaker*
Creative Speaking, *Frank*
Dynamics of Speech, *Myers & Herndon*
Getting Started in Oral Interpretation, *Naegelin & Krikac*
Getting Started in Public Speaking, *Carlin & Payne*
Listening by Doing, *Galvin*
Literature Alive, *Gamble & Gamble*
Person to Person, *Galvin & Book*
Public Speaking Today, *Carlin & Payne*
Speaking by Doing, *Buys, Sill, & Beck*

Theatre
Acting & Directing, *Grandstaff*
The Book of Cuttings for Acting & Directing, *Cassady*
The Book of Monologues for Aspiring Actors, *Cassady*
The Book of Scenes for Acting Practice, *Cassady*
The Book of Scenes for Aspiring Actors, *Cassady*
The Dynamics of Acting, *Snyder & Drumsta*
Getting Started in Theatre, *Pinnell*
An Introduction to Modern One-Act Plays, *Cassady*
An Introduction to Theatre and Drama, *Cassady & Cassady*
Play Production Today, *Beck et al.*
Stagecraft, *Beck*

For a current catalog and information about our complete line of
language arts books, write:
National Textbook Company
a division of NTC Publishing Group
4255 West Touhy Avenue
Lincolnwood (Chicago), Illinois 60646–1975 U.S.A.